Sinai and the Monastery of St. Catherine

SINAI

and the Monastery of St. Catherine

John Galey

Introductions by Kurt Weitzmann and George Forsyth

Doubleday & Company, Inc.
Garden City, New York
1980

© 1979 by Belser AG für Verlagsgeschäfte & Co. KG,
Stuttgart and Zürich for the German language edition.

© 1980 by Massada/Pelmas Ltd., Givatayim, Israel,
for the English language edition.

Book design: Hermann Kiesling, Stuttgart
Color separations: Schwitter AG, Basel
Composition: Knauer Layoutsatz GmbH, Stuttgart and
                Peli Printing Works Ltd., Givatayim
Colorplates printed by Amilcare Pizzi s.p.a.—arti grafiche,
                                Cinisello Balsamo, (Milano)
Textplates printed by Peli Printing Works Ltd., Givatayim

PRODUCED IN ISRAEL
by Peli Printing Works Ltd.

ISBN 0-385-17110-2
Library of Congress Catalog Card Number: 80-951

Dedication

"And the Lord said: draw not nigh hither:
put off thy shoes from off thy feet for
the place whereon thou standest is holy ground!"

(Exodus 3, 5)

This book is dedicated to the Sinai Expedition of the Universities of Michigan and Princeton, USA, as well as of the University of Alexandria, Egypt. Special thanks are due to my friends: Professor Kurt Weitzmann, Princeton, Professor George Forsyth, Michigan, Fred Anderegg, Michigan.

I had the good fortune to participate as photographer in this Expedition. A total of five months at the Monastery of St. Catherine culminated in thousands of photos. Two scientific research publications of this material from the Monastery of St. Catherine have appeared but are already out of print: G. Forsyth / K. Weitzmann, *The Church and the Fortress of Justinian* and K. Weitzmann, *The Icons, Volume I, 6th–10th Century*. This book is an outgrowth of my photographic material. I worked closely with Kurt Weitzmann whose special field is icon paintings. I am particularly grateful to him for his generous and active assistance. His contribution was invaluable to the creation of this book. Many thanks are also due to George Forsyth who put at my disposal his article on the architecture, history and plans of the Monastery. Thanks must also go to Fred Anderegg, the chief photographer from Michigan, who has since become one of my best friends. The Bedouins in Sinai call him "Mister Fred" and his hearty laughter is known throughout the desert. I would not wish to omit mentioning the work contributed by "guest members" of our expedition. These included Ihor Ševčenko of Dumbarton Oaks, USA, Ahmed Fikry and Samy Shenouda of Alexandria and Ernest Hawkins from England who restored the large mosaic.

May I also express my thanks to the present Archbishop, his Holiness Damianos and to all the monks of the Monastery. There is no doubt that their goodwill and helpfulness contributed to the success of our work.

SINAI — a name that resounds with the echoes of the Old Testament and reverberates with meaning to the present day. To live within the walls of this 1400–year old Monastery is to feel an indescribable fascination. The months spent at Sinai changed my life. May this book serve as a symbol of reconciliation and help remove prejudices among the Religions which have fed at the "springs" of Sinai — Judaism, Christianity and Islam. It is my sincere desire that the Monastery of St. Catherine in Sinai which has, in the course of centuries, withstood and survived so many dangers undamaged, be preserved for all time.

John Galey
Summer, 1979.

CONTENTS

Kurt Weitzmann

The History

Visitors to the monastery have frequently asked me: "How can we be sure that Moses and the Israelites were at this very spot in the rocky desert and that it was this very peak above the monastery where Moses received the tablets of the law?" My answer has always been to proffer the following historical considerations: When, sometime during the second millennium B.C., Moses wandered through Sinai after the exodus, the peninsula was in the hands of the Egyptians. But they lost control over it after the invasion of the Bedouins, nomads with no literary records. Obviously, then, when the Early Christians began to interest themselves in the Holy Sites of Palestine — and this includes Sinai, situated in what was then called Palestina Tertia — there were no written or oral traditions alive and thus they were neither helped nor hindered by previous guesswork about the places mentioned in the Book of Exodus. With a Bible in their hands the pilgrims set out from Egypt and identified places like that of the bitter water of Marah, the wells and palm trees of Elim and so forth. Yet there has been some dispute in modern scholarship as to which peak the first pilgrims considered to be the one on which Moses received the tablets. According to some it was the imposing, craggy ridge of Djebel Serbal, halfway up to the present monastery. At the foot of it lies the luscious Oasis of Faran, a bishopric in the fourth century. Seen almost from sea level this mountain looks much more impressive and convincing as the abode of Jaweh than the Djebel Mousa, the Moses mountain, which one can see only after one has reached a plateau at the height of 5000 feet, i.e.

the level of the present monastery. Moreover, for a considerable number of people to survive for several years in an inhospitable rocky desert is unthinkable without a sufficient supply of water and this was available only at the Oasis of Faran. Yet regardless of how one evaluates the rival claims between Djebel Serbal and Djebel Mousa, it was the latter that won out in the course of the fourth century.

At the end of that century, the noble lady Etheria, the first Sinai pilgrim of whom we have a record, and her entourage visited what no doubt are the present sites connected with the Burning Bush and the Receiving of the Law. These are her words: "There were many cells of holy men there, and a church in the place where the bush is... There is a very pleasant garden in front of the church, containing excellent and abundant water, and the Bush itself is in the garden. The spot is shown hardby, where holy Moses stood when God said to him: 'Lose the latchet of thy shoe.'"

In the sixth century the monks who had settled there and formed a loose community and who were being harassed by the local Bedouins sent a petition to Justinian, asking to have a monastery built for them. The emperor, interested as much in the security of the outer frontiers of the empire as in propagating the faith, granted their request and built a monastery with the stability of a fortress. Nearby, moreover, he settled a colony of mercenaries for the monastery's protection. According to tradition these mercenaries, were later to intermarry, with the local Bedouins, forming the tribe of the Djebeliye who, though having become Mohammedans, still serve the monastery today. Procopius, Justinian's court historian, has this to say about the monastery's foundation in his *De Aedificiis:* "A precipitous and terribly wild mountain, Sina by name, rears its height close to the Red Sea... On this Mount Sina live monks, whose life is a kind of careful rehearsal of death, and they enjoy without fear the solitude which is very precious to them... The emperor Justinian built them a church which he dedicated to the Mother of God so that they might be enabled to pass their lives therein, praying and holding services." The first century of the monastery's existence, founded late in the monarch's life (between 548 and 565) was, no doubt, its most flourishing period.

When the Muslims conquered Egypt, and therewith Sinai, in 640 A.D., the ties with Constantinople were temporarily severed and the monastery became more dependent of the patriarchate of Jerusalem, ties which exist to the present day. More often than not the new archbishop of the autocephalous Sinaitic Church was and still is enthroned by the patriarch of Jerusalem. In general, Muslims have a better record of religious tolerance than Christians, as is best proven by the fact that the monastery, a Christian enclave within Islamic territory, has an unbroken tradition. Moreover, the monastery belonged to the whole of Christendom and there were times when other orthodox monks, Syrians and Christian Arabs resided there. In about the tenth century a colony of Georgian monks played a considerable role.

Of course there were occasional persecutions of the Christians, the best known being that by a mystic, the unpredictable Caliph al-Hakim around the year 1000. When, according to tradition he set out to destroy the monastery, among other Christian buildings, the monks met him halfway and implored him to save it because it was also a holy place for Muslims and included a mosque within its walls — to bolster their plea they built a mosque in record time! This story seems to substantiate the architectural history of the mosque which had obviously originated as a two-story building and served some other purposes. Ties with Constantinople were resumed when Byzantine armies advanced close to Jerusalem in the tenth century; there is archaeological evidence pointing to this fact. After the end of iconoclasm in 843, icons and illustrated manuscripts in the style of the capital reached the monastery, asserting Constantinople's role as the arbiter of all religious, cultural and artistic matters within the orthodox world. Yet some of the renewed influences reached Sinai indirectly, mainly from the island of Cyprus. It had been reconquered in the tenth century by the imperial armies, and boasted of a rich Byzantine heritage. The monastery had, and still has, strong ties with the island since it owns several estates there, so-called *metochia*.

At about the same time, presumably in the tenth and at the latest in the eleventh century, the relics of Saint Catherine which had been reposited in a chapel at the peak of Djebel Katrin — higher even than that of Djebel Mousa — were transferred into the monastery. Thus Saint Catherine, whose body according to legend had originally been brought to Sinai by angels after her martyrdom at Alexandria, became the title saint of the monastery, which had been dedicated to the Virgin when it was built.

But the ties with Constantinople were to be broken again during the time of the crusades. In the twelfth century crusaders seem to have come only as visitors, but in the thirteenth century a colony of Latin monks resided in the monastery. They built their own chapel which became known as "Saint Catherine's of the Franks" and among the monks were artists who painted icons obviously for their own chapel. The monastery became integrated into the Latin patriarchate of Jerusalem and was placed under the jurisdiction of the suffragan bishop of Petra. This newly-established contact with the Latin West continued even after the collapse of the Crusader Kingdom because the autocephalous Church of Sinai had not taken part in the schism of 1054, which separated the Orthodox and the Roman Churches, and it had remained in communion with Rome. Sinai monks had gone to France to collect money and to sell relics and today the cathedral of Rouen possesses more relics of the body of Saint Catherine than the monastery itself which owns only the skull and one hand. Vice versa many pilgrims from the West, including noblemen and clerics, came to the monastery and one of the most striking evidences are the numerous coats of arms and names, carved — in some cases quite elaborately — into the walls of various buildings, but in particular into those of the refectory, the *trapeza,* where they must have taken their meals. The names and coats of arms are French, German, Dutch and English and the carvings are from the 14th — 16th centuries.

From the fall of Acre in 1291 marking the end of the Crusader Kingdom in the Holy Land, to the conquest of Constantinople by the Turks in 1453, the Palaeologan empire revitalized Byzantine culture and art and its influence was felt as far as Sinai. But even after the final disaster, Byzantine culture did not come to an end and the main center of what today is called the "post-Byzantine" era became the island of Crete. Here Byzantine art preserved its vitality even when the island was dominated by the Venetians. On Crete, as on Cyprus, Sinai had and still has today rich possessions, particularly in Heraclion, a flourishing metochion. Many icon painters from Crete worked on a large scale in Saint Catherine's.

Yet, along with the Greeks of Crete, the Slavs also laid claim to being heirs of Byzantium; the first to do so were the Gospodars of Moldavia and Valachia. Living close to the conquered capital they had gotten hold of some of its treasures, especially liturgical objects and they set out to establish workshops of their own that continued the tradition of the capital. A great many of these products were sent as gifts to major orthodox establishments, churches and especially monasteries, foremost among them Mount Athos, Jerusalem and Sinai. Soon, however, this role as protector of all Orthodoxy was contested by Moscow, the third Rome. Gifts from the Czar of Russia began to flood the Orthodox monasteries and the treasures of Athos, Jerusalem and Sinai are vivid testimony to these lavish gifts which, like the icons with rich metal coverings called oklad or riza, were often more ostentatious than artistic.

In spite of this strong Slavic influence at Sinai, the monastery's connection with the Latin West never broke off entirely. During the campaign of Napoleon in Egypt, he sent Marshal Kleber to the monastery to have its partly dilapidated walls restored and the library displays a document signed by Bonaparte in which he gives special privileges to the monastery.

As is clear from its history, Saint Catherine's belongs spiritually not only to the Greek, but also to a wider range of Orthodox churches like the Georgian, the Melchite Syrian, the Slavic, and at some time also the Roman. These are the Churches which adhere to the Chalcedonian dogma of the Two Natures of Christ, as formulated in the fourth ecumenical council of 451 A.D. More or less excluded are the so-called monophysite Churches, and this explains why there is hardly any influence from the Coptic Church, though Alexandria is so close, or from the Armenian. Sinai is part of the Holy Land and is one of its important Loca Sancta and therefore a goal of pilgrimages. But while most of the Holy Sites in Jerusalem, Bethlehem and Nazareth have again and again been destroyed or damaged by conquerors of various nationalities, Saint Catherine's monastery is the only one which has escaped destruction and which has been able to preserve an unparalleled heritage of Byzantine art and culture.

1 The Sinai peninsula, with the Gulf of Suez (left) and the Gulf of 'Aqaba (right). The Monastery of St. Catherine is situated in the mountain range in the lower section of the peninsula (Photo: NASA).

2 The 1,400-year-old monastery and garden at the foot of Mount Sinai as seen from the north-east.

5

6

3 The high walls en-
close an area of ap-
prox. 70×85 m. The
church is built along
the west-east axis.
Behind it and to the
right are guest quar-
ters. Chapels and
monks' living quarters
with their narrow al-
leys give it a villagelike
character.

4 The 12–15 m high
fortified wall built by
Justinian. The upper
part collapsed during
an earthquake in 1312.
It was restored in 1801
by Marshall Kléber on
Napoleon's instruc-
tions.

5 The medieval lift. In
those days all en-
trances at ground level
were blocked. Pilgrims
and provisions were
hauled up in nets and
baskets.

6 The winch is operat-
ed by four Bedouins.
The rope is slowly
reeled around the cen-
ter portion. A simple,
but reliable device.

7 The modern entrance gate as seen from outside (left). At right, the old, walled-up portal. The flat arch with its decorative roundels can be clearly seen.

8 A section of the well-kept north-east wall walk.

9 The modern entrance gate as seen from within. It was built in 1861 under Archbishop Kyrillos of Constantinople.

10 Stonemasonry on
the exterior of the
south-west wall
(height approx.
130 cm). Sixth
century.

11 Frescoes with bird
motives on the roof of
the small chapel in the
outer south-west wall.

12 Inside the sixth-
century chapel in the
outer wall.

13 The sixth-century church, an early Christian basilica, seen from the south-east. At right is the church tower built in 1871, behind it is the mosque. In the background is the twentieth-century guest wing with its dome-shaped stair-case.

14

14 Alley along the
north wall of the
church with the quar-
ters of the head monks
(left). This way leads
behind the church to
the site of the Burning
Bush.

15 Narrow streets,
chapels and buildings.
In the foreground, the
roof of the water pump
house.

5

16

17

18

16 Buildings in the south-east corner. The old library can be seen above the church (below right).

17 The Semandron, a wooden block, is struck by a hammer to call the monks to service.

18 A bell in the north-east corner of the monastery.

19 The mosque, built at the beginning of the twelfth century, with minaret. Thus the Islamic faith is also represented in the monastery.

20 Father Dionysius sitting before the holy site of the Burning Bush where God appeared before Moses.

21 Father Jeremias retires to his cell after attending service.

22 This picture was taken at night from the roof of the guest wing. The scant light is provided by the monastery generator which is turned off at 10 p. m. Afterwards petroleum lamps have to be used.

23, 24 Two details of
hardwood carvings in a
massive pew. The
work was carried out
by Procopius, a monk
from Caesarea and
Sinai, in 1784.
A nymphlike figure
(23) beneath the seat.
One foot of the pew in
the form of a lionlike
mythical animal (24).

25 Detail of the ex-
terior doors leading
into the church. They
are richly decorated
with carvings in
cypress. Together with
the narthex the doors
were made at the time
of the Fatimids, tenth
to twelfth century.

26 The huge main
portal, rich with wood
carvings, dating from
the founding of the
monastery in the sixth
century. It connects
the narthex with the
church. The portal is
3.63 m high and 2.40 m
wide and is made of
cypress.

23

24

25

27

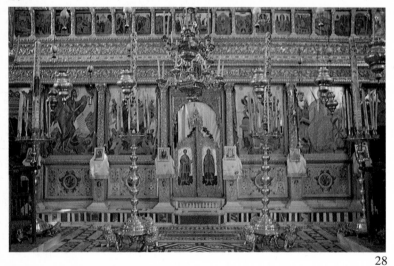

28

27 In the foreground is a huge chandelier, behind it are the carved beams of the sixth-century rafters. The green panels with their star motives are eighteenth century.

28 The gilded iconostasis in front of the altar. It came from Crete and was built in 1612 under Archbishop Laurentius.

29

29 The aluminium scaffolding, more than 10 m tall, which enabled us to photograph the roof beams as well as the mosaic in detail.

30 A view of the central aisle of the church with its chandeliers and ostrich eggs hanging from the roof.

31

32

31–33 Three details of the richly decorated beams, dating from Justinian times, with animal and plant elements.

34 These two inscriptions in the beams enabled exact dating of the monastery: "To the salvation of our pious emperor, Justinian," and "To the memory and the rest of the soul of our Em-press." Theodora died in 548 A. D. and Justinian in 565 A. D. The church must, therefore, have been built sometime between these dates.

35 The interesting
rafters construction.
The roof was originally
open and could be
seen from below.

35

36 View from the roof into the interior of the church. The marble and porphyry floor dates back to Archbishop Athanasios (1714). The original floor was destroyed by raiding Arabs in the sixteenth century while searching for buried treasure.

37 The high altar. Inlaid work in mother of pearl dating from Archbishop Ioannikios of Peloponnesos, 1675. The work was carried out by Stamatios of Athens.

38 The chapel of the Burning Bush. The holiest place in the monastery. Like Moses, the visitor has to take off his shoes before entering. There are valuable carpets on the floor and numerous icons on the walls. The fayence tiles on the walls and in the apse of the altar are from Damascus. Beneath the altar is a silver plate with an inscription dated 1696.

39 The tomb of Saint Catherine under a marble baldachin. The relics are kept here. Two richly engraved silver caskets contain the skull and a ringed hand of Saint Catherine. Silver oil lamps burn day and night above the tomb.

George H. Forsyth

The Monastery of St. Catherine at Mount Sinai: The Church and Fortress of Justinian

That the Monastery of St. Catherine exists at all can only be explained by its location. It stands near the center of the barren granitic mountains whose tumbled masses fill the lower reaches of the Sinai Peninsula, forming an almost impenetrable fastness between Africa and Asia. Like the Thebaid, it provided a secure retreat for the hermits who established [1] the monastic tradition of the Peninsula. But at the same time, these devious and obscure gorges gave shelter to a very different kind of activity. For millennia the desert tribes of Arabia have used the Sinai Mountains as a covert for infiltrating Palestine. This is the reason for the fortress-like [2-5] quality of the monastery.

The monastery lies in the Wadi ed-Deir ("The Valley of the [49] Monastery") below a shoulder of Mt. Sinai. To the west the valley broadens out into the Plain of er-Raha, the traditional campground of the [48] Israelites. It was on this plain that the Israelites camped while Moses communed with God on the summit of the Mountain. There is no absolute certainty that this is the actual Mount of the Decalogue. The Jews, after settling in Palestine, lost all track of their former wanderings. Since the fourth century however, this mountain, Gebel Musa, has been accepted as the true and sacred one. The spot where the monastery now stands has been revered as the site of the Burning Bush. Towards the close of the fourth century the location was visited by Etheria, whose travel diary, the *Peregrinatio,* has survived and is a mine of information concerning Jerusalem and other sacred places in the Holy Land and in the Near East.

Etheria's careful record of her travels includes an account of her visit to Mt. Sinai.[1] She describes in detail her ascent of the back of the mountain, whereon she passed a night, and her descent on its eastern side. The path she followed led her to the site of the Burning Bush which, she says, "is alive to this day and throws out shoots."

Although the monastery of Justinian would not be built here for another century and a half, its basic pattern as the place where the sacred Bush, stood, tended by an eremitical group who maintained an adjoining church and welcomed pilgrims, was established already. The architectural program was essentially complete — save for one feature, defense.

According to various accounts, the holy men of the mountain who welcomed Etheria at the Burning Bush were shortly thereafter subjected to persecutions and massacres by wild tribes. The accounts are unreliable and indeed, seem largely fictitious, but they may contain authentic echoes of that restless movement of peoples along the eastern marches of the later Roman Empire, like besiegers testing the defenses of a fortress. Under Justinian and his predecessors, an elaborate defensive system had been erected to counter such threats. Extending all the way from Armenia to the borders of Egypt, its northern sector was designed to withstand onslaughts of the redoubtable Sassanians from Persia and its southern part was intended to blunt the fierce raids of the desert peoples.

2-4   The present fortified monastery at the foot of Mt. Sinai appears to have been erected by Justinian as a part of this defensive system. According to a later account, he built it merely to protect the monks; but Procopius says in his book *On the Buildings* (De Aedificiis) written at about the same time, that its function as a fortress was primarily to prevent the Saracens from making surprise attacks upon Palestine from this uninhabited region.

"Emperor Justinian built this church, not on the mountain's summit, but much lower down. For it is impossible for a man to pass the night on

50

the summit, since constant crashes of thunder and other terrifying manifestations of divine power are heard at night, striking terror into man's body and soul. It was in that place, they say, that Moses received the laws from God and published them. And at the base of the mountain this Emperor built a very strong fortress and established there a considerable garrison of troops, in order that the barbarian Saracens might not be able from that region, which, as I have said, is uninhabited, to make inroads with complete secrecy into the lands of Palestine proper."[2]

It must be admitted that Procopius' account, taken by itself, is not very satisfactory. He mentions the church, then the mountain on which Moses received the laws from God, and finally the fortress at its base. From this description one might conclude that the church and the fortress, being mentioned separately, were located at a distance from each other. Fortunately the church, surrounded by fortress walls, bears its own documentation in the form of an inscription of Justinian carved on a beam over its nave. [34]

There is no other fortress in the region. Clearly, then, Procopius refers to the church with its fortress.

Moreover, it is curious that Procopius makes no mention of the Burning Bush or of pilgrims to its site. Indeed, he stresses the solitude of the monks which, as he says, is "very precious to them." In Procopius' account the main emphasis is placed on the monks and on the Saracens, so that Justinian's foundation would appear to have been both monastic and military in character. Fortunately, the layout of the monastery church itself tells us it was designed to function as a center of pilgrimage — of pilgrimage to an outdoor relic, doubtless a growing bush as in Etheria's day. This can be verified by examining the east end of the church. At present, the area behind the main apse is occupied by the Chapel of the Burning Bush, so called because its altar stands over a slab which marks the site of the Bush. Access to the chapel is through doors from two [38]

51

neighboring chapels which are at the ends of the church aisles and which jut well beyond the main apse. The relation between the three chapels is clear in the plan (fig. 1). As viewed from the exterior, the roof of the Burning Bush Chapel appears as a flat surface sloping down from the three-sided housing of the main apse and flanked by the domes which cover the two adjoining chapels.

Originally there was no Burning Bush Chapel but, in its stead, a small open area at the foot of the main apse, like a diminutive court or open bay, accessible through the two doors from the adjoining chapels. In the court was the Bush itself.

Evidently the present Chapel of the Burning Bush is later than the church because it projects beyond the corner chapels and overlaps them. The lines of reprise are clear and unquestionable. The exact date when the Bush was replaced by the chapel is unknown, but it must have been before 1216. In that year a German pilgrim, Magister Thietmar, visited Sinai: "There is also in a chapel of this monastery the spot where stood the bush venerated by all, as much by Saracens as by Christians... The bush has indeed been taken away and divided among Christians for relics."[3]

In spite of Procopius' description of the fortress as "very strong," it does not appear quite as formidable as his phrase suggests.

Standing at the base of a slope, its walls could have been dominated by archers from the heights above. While its vulnerable position was, of course, dictated by the site of the Burning Bush near the bottom of the valley, the puzzling fact remains that Byzantine military engineers, famous for their skill in fortification and siegecraft, should have been content to encircle the fortress by a wall without effective flanking towers. Those on the lower side, facing northeast, are relatively modern; the original ones on the upper, southwest side project too little to provide enfilading fire along the curtain wall, but originally they were higher so as to dominate the rampart-walk. Probably such a fortress was adequate to awe the desert

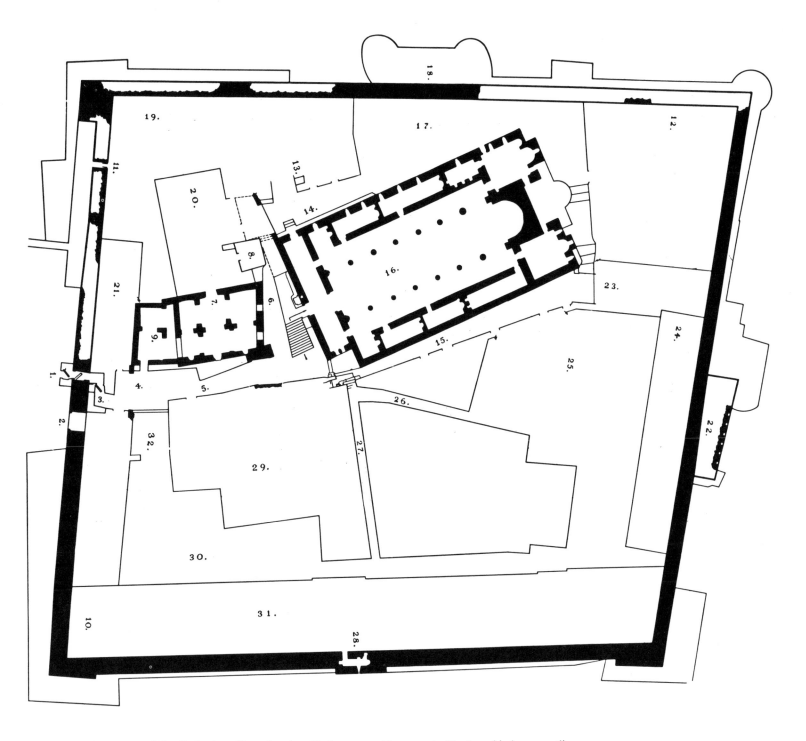

Mt. Sinai, Monastery of St. Catherine. Plan showing Sixth-century Elements in black and in heavy outline

1. Porch (originally, Postern)
2. Original Portal (blocked)
3. Entry (under Guest Wing)
4. Court
5. Covered Psssage (Mediaeval Vault)
6. Court and Steps down to Church
7. Mosque (Converted Sixth-century Guest House)
8. Minaret
9. Storeroom (Sixth-century Antechamber)
10. Complex of Sixth-century Arches in Basement at West Corner
11. Rainwater Drain (Sixth Century) running Northwest under Road and to Garden

12. Modern Kitchen and Service Quarters in East Corner (above Sixth-century Kitchen)
13. Well of Moses
14. Uncovered Passage at Lower Level
15. Uncovered Passage at Upper Level
16. Church
17. Court
18. Kléber's Tower (Early Nineteenth Century)
19. Modern Living Quarters and Reception Room of Head Monks, in North Corner
20. Terrace (on Sixth-century Arches)
21. Guest Wing (Nineteenth Century)
22. Former Latrine Tower in Southeast Wall

23. Present Refectory (Mediaeval)
24. Modern Living Quarters of Monks (against Southeast Wall) communication by Verandahs
25. Court above Modern Bakery
26. Tunnel under 29
27. Tunnel under 29
28. Chapel (Sixth Century) in Southwest Wall
29. Structures of Various Uses and Dates (post Sixth Century)
30. Court (Well at Center)
31. Modern Building of Sixth-century Wall
32. Ramp Mounting from 4

53

tribesmen. Indeed, Procopius explains the modest fortification wall with the remark that "the Saracens are naturally incapable of storming a wall and the weakest kind of barricade, put together with perhaps nothing but mud, is sufficient to check their assault."[4]

The original outer wall can be traced through its whole perimeter, in spite of later remodellings and superstructures. On three sides it rises impressively to its original height. In many places its battlements are still in position. At the center of the southeast wall is the latrine tower, largely reconstructed in later periods.

Obviously the architect was greatly inconvenienced by the location of the site of the Burning Bush which, like any holy spot, could not possibly be moved. Since it was located only a short distance up the slope from the runoff for the entire valley, where flash floods sometimes occur, he was unable to dispose the square plan of the fortress around the Burning Bush site as its central focus, which would have been a more obvious arrangement. To do so would have been to risk destruction of that part of the fortress which would extend into the runoff. In his effort to avoid such an exposed position, the architect erected the square as far up the slope as possible, accepting a lopsided composition wherein the site of the Bush is in one corner of the square and in its lowest part.[5]

The best preserved of the fortress walls is on the south-west side, beneath an enormous modern structure which occupies that whole flank of the monastery. At various places in the original circuit, especially at its corners, large glacis of rubble have been added during periods when the wall seemed precarious, perhaps due to earthquakes. All the masonry is of granite, the only building material available locally.[6]

The main entrance of the monastery was in its western wall and consisted of a large, imposing portal, now walled up. To the left of it is the present entrance, a low postern, preceded by an eighteenth century porch. The portal was crowned by a flat arch with decorative roundels at each

54

end and must have been closed by a massive door.

No doubt it was reserved for formal entry on important occasions, while the postern was used for ordinary comings and goings.

From the entrance of the monastery the route to be followed by pilgrims to the Burning Bush is clearly indicated by the architecture itself. The route leads to the church, then goes along an aisle of the church and out into the former court of the Burning Bush, now the chapel of that name, and then back through the other aisle, thereby completing within the church a circuit in the form of the letter U, around the back of the apse.

In order to follow the above route a pilgrim would enter the main portal of the monastery, or the adjoining postern, passing underneath a porch beyond which was an unroofed passage. This led to a simple arched propylaeum with a view of the corner of the church beyond.

On the north side of the unroofed passage was the guest house, originally a two-story oblong structure entered from the west through a one-story annex. Surprisingly enough, in the eleventh century this structure was converted into a mosque. Sufficient head room was obtained by removing the upper floor, and the necessary niches were inserted in the south wall to indicate the direction of Mecca. The assumption has always been that the building was erected as a mosque, but there is ample archaeological evidence of its sixth century date and of its original form and purpose before it was remodelled. There are visible sills of doors, which once connected the second-story rooms, and traces of the floor which formerly abutted under the sills. Two doors, now blocked up, led from the guest house to the small triangular court in front of the church. Tradition has it that the "Turkish" general of an invading army sent advance notice to the monks of his intention to reach the monastery in three days time and then to destroy it and, further, that the monks frantically "built" the mosque before the arrival of the general on the assumption that a good Moslem, would spare the monastery for its sake

19

55

— an assumption which proved correct (see Kurt Weitzmann's introduction). Whether or not there is any basis of fact in the story, the facts are odd: a mosque was "built" by converting a building as important as the guest house and seemingly with careless haste, this can be seen by the very inferior construction of the minaret. The mosque (but not the minaret) is still used for the benefit of Moslem guests and for the Bedouin servants of the monastery. To the right of the main portal, an open space may have been reserved as a courtyard, unencumbered by buildings; at least, there is no trace of any early building in that area. As a place of pilgrimage, the monastery was in part a caravansary and may well have included within its sheltering walls, an open area for all the multitudinous activities of arriving and departing groups of pilgrims.

Continuing along the route from the portal of the monastery to the façade of the church, the visitor advances through the arched passageway and is surprised to find the church sunk deeply in the ground. As indicated by outcrops of live rock, this submergence is not due to a rise in ground level. Rather, it is caused by the fact that the site of the Burning Bush is in the lowest part of the whole monastery and, therefore, the floor of the adjoining church had to be established at about that level, a good four meters below the ground level of the portal of the monastery and of the approach from it to the church. A flight of steps leads from the upper level to the church door below; the steps are relatively modern but probably resemble the original flight.

In order to offset as much as possible the effect of submergence, the façade of the church is heightened by increasing the vertical proportions of its interior beyond the norm and by making the gables inordinately high, much higher than the roof ridge. The three-storied campanile was a gift from Russia nearly a century ago.

To the left of the steps leading down to the church is the wall of the mosque with its two blocked-up doors that once opened toward the church from that building when it was still a guest house. On entering the church at the right, the pilgrim would find himself in the Narthex. Facing him was the great inner door of the nave.

26,30

The nave with its lofty proportions is reminiscent of many Romanesque churches. The view is obstructed by chandeliers and a huge seventeenth century iconostasis, but originally the mosaic over the altar would have been visible for the full length of the nave.

28

The roof of the nave is carried by a series of thirteen trusses. Abundant evidence, including carbon-14 tests, guarantees that this sturdy structure has stood unaltered since the time of Justinian, It is centuries older than comparable wooden roofs existing elsewhere. From the fourteenth to the twentieth centuries it carried a lead sheathed roof, and very likely it did so as early as the sixth century.[7] The trusses were originally visible from the floor of the church, but since the eighteenth century wood panels have been suspended between the horizontal beams so as to produce a flat ceiling over the nave. The panels are flush with the bottom surfaces of the beams, thus preventing a person standing in the nave from seeing three inscriptions carved on the sides of three of the beams and which could once be read from below. The inscriptions are invocations on behalf of the Emperor Justinian, of his Empress Theodora, and of Stephanos of Aila, who was the builder of the church.[8] Since the first inscription implies that Justinian was still alive, while the second indicates that Theodora was already dead, the church must have been commissioned between 548 and 565. Since Procopius probably published the *Buildings* in about 560, the space of time may be narrowed to twelve years. It is a rare piece of good fortune that so well-preserved a church should be a signed and dated work. Luckily, the later panels were hung between the horizontal beams, not under them, and therefore do not conceal the bottom surfaces of the beams, on which sixth century carvings of floral ornament, animals, sea creatures and river scenes are still visible. At a later date they were

31–34

13

35

27, 29

34

57

highlighted with gold and red paint, enough of which has peeled off to
reveal the authenticity of the carvings, This remarkable series of relief
sculptures was executed with extraordinary verve and realism.

31–33

The second beam from the entrance shows a Nilotic scene; in the
center is a Cross, as on all the beams, and here it is flanked by tritons who
carry Crosses. The left and right halves are occupied by river animals,
plants and two boats, one being frantically propelled by two rowers,
probably *erotes,* and the other under sail. On another beam is a lively
frieze of animals, including a camel and an elephant. There are also
animated scenes of predators pursuing their quarry and of various
underwater creatures. Finally, the easternmost beam shows at its center a
Cross with confronted peacocks and in addition two bulls, a rabbit and a
gazelle. Such mundane subjects seem inappropriate to the sanctity of a
church, but they may be intended to convey a serious iconographic
message. They can be compared to floor mosaics such as the *mappa
mundi* which was found in a church of the same period. This "map" is a
representation of the terrestrial world and is described in the
accompanying inscription as "bearing round about in the skillful images of
art everything that breathes and creeps."[9] Such a caption would be highly
suitable for the Sinai beams, which attest to the competence and variety of
Early Byzantine sculpture.

The great door to the nave, also richly decorated with relief sculpture,

26

reveals the same high standards of quality as the beam carvings. Like the
beams, its lintel bears an inscription and its outer and inner surfaces are
enlivened by reliefs of beasts, birds and floral ornament. Paleographic and
stylistic resemblances guarantee that it is of the same period as the beams.
Such a door, with its four valves swung back, is a magnificent preface to
the lofty church and theophanic spot beyond it. Among the subjects on the
door panels are an eagle, a beautiful gazelle and a splendid strutting cock.

On passing through the door, one becomes more aware of the side aisles to left and right. In the sixth century the approach through the central door may not have been freely open to the ordinary lay pilgrim. At that time the side aisles, not the central nave, would probably have been considered the appropriate avenues of approach for pilgrims making their way to the Burning Bush; and they would have been admitted directly into the aisles through the two side doors provided for that purpose. The center door may have been reserved for the monks themselves, as well as for great visiting personages and high occasions, because it opened into the nave and shared the honor of that central space. The Orthodox Church treats the nave of a basilica as a westward extension of the area in which the liturgical offices are performed. We have abundant architectural and some documentary evidence that such was the case at least as far back as the sixth century.[10] Certainly it is true of modern services in the Mt. Sinai church.

Today, no lay person is prohibited from setting foot in the nave through the great western door, but this may not have been true originally.

If we imagine an ordinary pilgrim as being admitted from the Narthex into the interior of the church through the small door to the left of the great central one, he would see before him the perspective of the north aisle. On the right is the nave colonnade; on the left are doors to a row of chapels. Directly ahead is an opening in the eighteenth century iconostasis and, beyond that, a monumental bronze-sheathed door which was an important feature of the sixth century arrangements since its valves gave formal entrance to the corner chapel and thence to the court of the Burning Bush.

Before advancing along the aisle, the pilgrim might have stopped to examine the Chapel of Sts. Constantine and Helen.

This is roofed by a segmental tunnel vault of rubble, which replaces the original flat wood ceiling. Carried by beams resting on corbels, its end wall contains a large central niche with a smaller niche to the left. There is no doubt that this and the other similar chapels which flank the church on both sides formed part of the original plan, yet the large number of them and their orderly, balanced arrangement, such as an additional aisle on each side, are exceptional for the period. Normally, an Early Byzantine church had only a main altar and, at most, a couple of chapels, often placed asymmetrically. The arrangement here, however, is reminiscent of later monastic churches in the West, where multiple altars were required and where they might be disposed in orderly fashion along the aisles.

Frequently Justinian's churches were furnished with marble capitals and other decorative fittings which had been fully detailed at one of the Imperial marble quarries.[11] A few smaller examples are found here, but obviously the big nave capitals, nearly a meter high, had to be carved of local granite, the only building material in the vicinity. The quality varies greatly. Some have a rough-hewn vigor, expressive of their recalcitrant material and reminiscent of early Romanesque style. The pilgrimage route continues along the north aisle. On the right, passing through the opening in the iconostasis, is the chancel and high altar. In the foreground is a marble panel with a shallow relief representing two confronted deer flanking a Cross. As indicated above, the panel was probably carved in one of the Imperial marble quarries and imported to form part of the original chancel rail. At the center of the chancel the original marble altar table is preserved, a monumental structure composed of a great slab supported on six colonettes, the whole being encased in an eighteenth century housing of marquetry. On the far side of the chancel stands the tomb of St. Catherine. In part it is composed of re-used marble fragments, including another chancel panel and a small capital and colonette. These scattered fragments may have come from a chancel screen similar to contemporary examples found elsewhere. In the case of the church, at Sinai the chancel would have occupied only the last bay of the nave because its two columns are considerably thicker than the rest, suggesting their greater importance as marking the limits of the chancel. Such

37

39

60

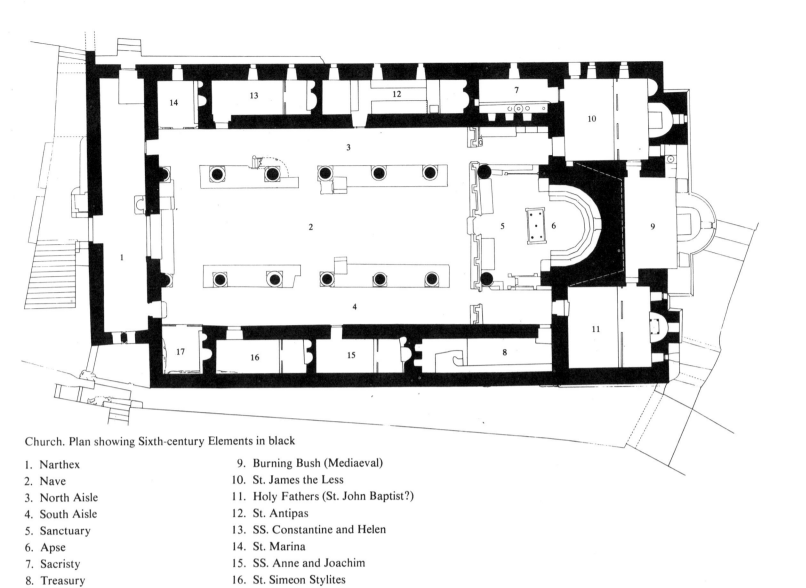

Church. Plan showing Sixth-century Elements in black

1. Narthex
2. Nave
3. North Aisle
4. South Aisle
5. Sanctuary
6. Apse
7. Sacristy
8. Treasury
   Chapels in Church

9. Burning Bush (Mediaeval)
10. St. James the Less
11. Holy Fathers (St. John Baptist?)
12. St. Antipas
13. SS. Constantine and Helen
14. St. Marina
15. SS. Anne and Joachim
16. St. Simeon Stylites
17. SS. Cosmas and Damian

transverse colonnades, appearing already in the sixth century, are the prototypes of the iconostasis screen.

Finally, in the apse vault above the altar and on the wall above the vault appear the series of mosaic pictures which are the greatest treasure of the monastery. They are, as mosaics, a part of the wall of the church, just as much as the marble revetment below them. Therefore, their formal design can be studied as part of the architectural design of the interior of the church. Moreover, being placed above the sanctuary and hence at the very focus toward which all lines of the nave converge, they surely express the theme which gives peculiar meaning to this church and are relevant, therefore, to its intended function. The mosaics have both a formal and a functional aspect.

119–136

The theme is primarily the Transfiguration, as represented in the apse, and secondarily, Moses at Mt. Sinai, receiving his mission at the Burning Bush, in the top left panel, and receiving the Tablets of the Law, in the top
right panel. Moses is a unifying link since he was also present at the Transfiguration, "talking with Jesus." And not only he but also Elijah, another Old Testament figure associated with Mt. Sinai. Both of them are here present in the apse mosaic, standing to left and right of Christ.

The special function of the church is, therefore, clearly indicated in the mosaic. In addition to the normal liturgical purpose, for which the church was given to the monks, it was intended to commemorate the Transfiguration, This commemorative aspect of the church's function is magnificently illustrated at the head of the church toward which the axis of the nave firmly directs the visitor.

The pictorial theme is carefully adapted to the formal requirements of its architectural setting. Seen from the nave, the half dome of the apse appears like a great eye of which the mandorla of Christ is the pupil. Elijah and Moses standing to left and right, the kneeling figures of John and James, and the recumbent Peter under the mandorla are all harmonized within the architectural motif which, through the power of its abstract design, reinforces the pictorial message and gives it a symphonic impact. The two rows of medallions, which outline the apse like an architectural frieze, contain portraits of Old Testament figures below and New Testament ones above so that, again, the architectural design and the
pictorial message blend to reinforce each other. Likewise, the two winged figures above perform the double function of filling the spandrels of the arch and of offering the scepter and orb to the Lamb, which occupies a medallion in the keystone position. Between them, providing a visual link between the medallion of the Lamb and the mandorla of Christ, is another medallion which contains, as a symbolic link, the Cross. Such perfect blending of didactic and architectural arts, each reinforcing the other, is an

extraordinary example of significant form.

The same fusion of form and content is evident in details of the mosaic. In the head and bust of Christ the simplified forms with emphatically rounded contours have an architectural character suited to their location in the curved half dome of the apse. In turn this simplification reduces the image to its expressive essentials, conveying through the power of abstract design an overwhelming effect of transcendent majesty. 120

The ornamental details are also of interest. In the double window over the apse the glazing is post-Byzantine, but the surrounding mosaic ornament is original. Especially noteworthy is the impressionistic rendering of the leaves of the capital. The pilgrim's route then leads through the bronze-sheathed door and into the northeast chapel.

This is one of the two symmetrical chapels at the east end of the church, both entered from the aisles through bronze doors and both covered with domes which are conspicuous from the exterior. Beyond the small iconostasis within the chapel is a door on the right which leads into the Chapel of the Burning Bush. As noted earlier, this was once an exterior door opening onto a small court in which grew the bush venerated as the original Burning Bush of Moses. Passing through the door one enters the chapel erected in the Middle Ages to replace the bush which, according to Thietmar, had been "taken away and divided among Christians for relics." At present a marble slab under the altar marks the spot where it once 38 flourished. It is worth recapitulating the route taken by the pilgrims within the church. They were conducted along one aisle and, after visiting the Bush, would naturally complete their tour by moving back along the other aisle. Their path to the relic would therefore be in the form of a U around the back of the main apse. Such a subordinate position for the Bush and such a circuitous route to it indicate its secondary importance. The principal focus of the church is the main apse which terminates the axis of the nave. We must conclude, therefore, that in spite of the renown of the

Sinai pilgrimage the monastic establishment, represented by the nave, was even more important. Implicit in the plan of the church is a basic distinction of attitude. To the ordinary pilgrim the Burning Bush was a numinous object which he viewed with awe and wonder and then went on his way with faith renewed by a witness so tangible For the monks in their nave, however, the Burning Bush was evidently just a local memento, a reminder, of the unfolding of God's plan of salvation, so subtly and powerfully set forth in the mosaic over their main altar. Between the relic and the mosaic is only a wall, the wall of the main apse, but in idea they are very far apart.[12] There are many more structures and features of the sixth century monastery which still survive, such as the intricate arrangements for drainage and conservation of water, the diminutive chapel in the thickness of the southwest wall, the vast arcading under the terraces, and the original kitchen, oven, and vault for storage of food. Although intrinsically interesting, they are less important than the fortress and the church. The determination and the administrative ability displayed in the construction of the monastery at Mt. Sinai bear eloquent witness to the disciplined vigor of Eastern Christendom under Justinian, while the sheer physical achievement of implanting this sophisticated structure in a howling wilderness, partly built of recalcitrant local granite and partly of materials imported with infinite toil, commands our greatest respect.

40 The pilgrims' route of 3,000 steps begins behind the monastery and leads up to Mount Sinai.

41 Halfway to Horeb is this small plateau with a huge old cypress. In the background is the chapel of Elijah.

42

42 The small church on the top of Mount Sinai. It is built of red granite blocks. They probably come from a much older church which used to stand on this holy site.

43 The gateway of St. Stephanos. Here he heard pilgrims' confessions and kept watch.

44 The magnificent Sinai scenery. Red granite formed by wind and weather many thousand years ago.

45 An hour away from the monastery, on the way to "Arba'in." This rock with its 12 notches (on the way to the monastery of the Forty Martyrs) is supposed to be the rock Moses struck water from. The 12 notches symbolize the 12 tribes of Israel.

46 The present approach to the monastery with the garden in the foreground.

47 Between the monastery and the Plain of El-Raha on a small hill is the chapel of Aaron. It is here that the golden calf is supposed to have stood.

48 View from the monastery terrace. In the foreground the garden. The way leads past the chapel of Aaron to the Plain of El-Raha where the people of Israel made camp.

49 Looking west from the chapel of Theodora. The monastery lies in the valley, like a sand castle in this gigantic landscape. At left, the foot of Mount Sinai.

50 The ascent to Mount Catherine, 2,800 m above sea level. The camels safely tread the small tracks brinking deep ravines. The remains of Saint Catherine were found on this mountain.

51 Following a difficult and hot climb by foot I was rewarded by this extraordinary view of the monastery from the north-east.

Kurt Weitzmann

The Arts

The visitor, entering the great basilica — the focal point of the monastery — may at first glance be slightly bewildered. In its original state he would immediately have been attracted by and drawn to the apse and its dominating mosaic. Now his view is blocked by the high iconostasis of the 17th century with a crowning painted monumental crucifix reaching almost to the ceiling. Moreover, huge bronze chandeliers, manufactured in 30 the 18th century in Nuremberg, make it difficult to get even a good view of the iconostasis itself. The whitewashed walls and the covering of the twelve supporting columns of the nave with plaster give a cold impression. Yet, patient scrutiny and a discerning eye will discover that more of the old furnishing and decoration has survived than the first impression would seem to indicate.

At the entrance, the huge portal, almost 4 meters high, with double folding valves looms before us. It is one of the very few wooden doors of the Early Christian period to have survived, being obviously the original one of Justinian's church and the best preserved in existence. The perfect state of preservation is due in part to the intricate insertion of the 28 panels within grooves of the framing beams, which prevent their removal, and consequently not a single one has been lost. Four of the panels at middle height are filled with vines emerging from a cantharos and they may well be understood as allusions to the eucharistic chalice. Others, with peacocks for example, represent well known Christian symbols. But otherwise the decoration which includes plants and animals of all kinds,

81

even an ape, is still much in the tradition of late classical pagan art.

Still standing in the entrance and looking up at the ceiling the eye catches huge panels of rather recent vintage inserted between the beams. But one day while standing on the high scaffold so that I could touch the ceiling I noticed that the undersides of the wooden beams were carved with reliefs in very much the same style as the door and that, consequently, we were face to face with a unique feature, the original 6th century roof. The thirteen beams show a great wealth of ornamental motifs and here the mixture of the classical tradition with Christian symbols is even more striking than in the portal. The centers of the beams show the Christian cross within a wreath, flanked in some cases by peacocks or the vine, suggesting the same Christian symbolism as in the door. But in other beams the crosses are flanked by crocodiles and the flora and fauna of the Nile, including putto rowing in boats. There are even sea monsters with human upper bodies, carrying cross-staffs — a rather unusual mixture of pagan and Christian elements. There are birds, quadrupeds hunting each other, aquatic creatures and so forth. The modern paint in gold and red may well have been one of the reasons why these carvings had hitherto not been recognized as some of the most important wood sculptures of the Early Christian period. Three of the beams have on their front sides, now invisible because of the later panels in between, inscriptions carved in huge letters. One day we removed temporarily one of the panels and standing on the floor of the church we could easily read these inscriptions in capital letters with the naked eye. The first implores the salvation of our pious emperor Justinian, and the second the memory and the rest of the soul of our empress Theodora. They clearly indicate that the church was roofed in the lifetime of Justinian, but after the death of Theodora, i. e. between the years 548 and 565, a date which must then be applied also to the wooden door. The third inscription, of equal interest, mentions a certain Stephanos of Aila as the architect and craftsman of the church — a rather unique

82

signature of an architect on a building of the Early Christian period. Aila where the architect came from is the present Aqaba close to the southern tip of Jordan.

In passing through the nave the visitor will notice that in one place the plaster covering of the columns has been chipped off and that underneath exist monolithic granite columns; also the capitals, now over-painted in an ugly green color, are of granite. It is hard to realize now the original impression of solidity and warmth of color that the granite must have given.

One also must realize that at the end of the nave where the high wooden iconostasis now stands, there was one of marble with low chancel panels of which two with the common motif of deers flanking the cross on the hill of Golgotha, still exist within the Sanctuary. Most likely this first iconostasis consisted of a structure of marble pillars supporting a marble architrave, but not yet including painted icons between the pillars; probably there were curtains which may well have been painted. In any event this structure was fairly low so that it did not obstruct the view into the apse with its mosaic decoration.

In the Sanctuary the focal point is of course the altar now covered on all four sides by 17th century marquetry under a high baldachin in the same technique. But opening this wooden structure at the rear and looking inside reveals the old marble altar resting on marble columns. The tomb of St. Catherine, to the right, is an 18th century marble structure under a baldachin and one wonders what the original depository of her relics may have looked like after the saint's body was transferred from the little chapel on the peak of Djebel Katrin to the monastery in about the 10th century.

The most attractive and intact part within the sanctuary is the revetment with marble whose grain is used to the greatest advantage by the architect to create symmetrical patterns. In the midst of the marble

37

presbyter bench rises the old bishop's throne, likewise of marble. With the transfer of the bishop's throne into the nave where now a sumptuously carved wooden one of the 18th century stands, the marble seat was deprived of its original function and now holds a tabernacle also in marble, for the host.

129, 136 The conch above this beautiful revetment is filled with the most outstanding mosaic left to us from the Early Christian period, depicting the Transfiguration of Christ on Mount Tabor. Its first impression is overpowering due to the truly monumental scale of its figures and the lucidity of its composition. This monumentality is created by the strong symmetry — with Christ standing on the axis in a strictly frontal view in an aureola with radiating silver rays. Moses and Elijah stand at either side and the three disciples who had gone with Christ to Mount Tabor, John, James and Peter, are placed on the ground. There were various reasons for choosing this subject as the focal point of the church. One is because of its association with the Second Coming, as suggested by the church father John Chrysostom, who says in a homily: "Hereafter He shall come in the very glory of the Father, not with Moses and Elijah only, but with the infinite host of the angels... not with a cloud over his head, but with heaven surrounding him." A major concern of Orthodoxy is the dogma of the Two Natures of Christ as formulated at the Ecumenical Council at Chalcedon in 451. What could be better proof of this dogma than the change from human to divine and back to human nature on Mount Tabor before the eyes of the three apostles who were present?

The Transfiguration is surrounded by busts of twelve Apostles and sixteen prophets, interrupted in the axis by a cross medallion at the top and the bust of David at the bottom — alluding once more to the Two Nature doctrine — and by two portraits in the corners, pulsing with character, of 136, 129 the energetic Abbot Longinus at the right and the very sensitive and ascetic Deacon John at the left. These are obviously the persons in whose

84

lifetime the mosaic was commissioned and executed. On the triumphal arch above, two angels offer orb and scepter to Christ, represented here in Early Christian fashion, a fashion later abandoned as the Lamb of God. On a Roman triumphal arch Victories had offered the same implements to the emperor and we see here once more to what extent Christian art was, in its pictorial repertory, indebted to the classical past. Underneath the flying angels are the medallion busts of John the Baptist whose face has the configurations of a tragic mask, a style befitting this tragic prophet, and the Virgin. The two represent the Old and New Dispensation, being the intercessors who together with Christ form what is called the Deesis, i.e. the Supplication. It is the earliest representation of this subject, which became very central in later Byzantine art.

Moving into the area above the conch of the apse one recognizes, left and right of a double window, Moses loosening the sandals before the Burning Bush and receiving the law — not in the usual shape of a double tablet but in the form of a scroll. The selection of these two scenes of Moses for the sanctuary has a long tradition reaching back into Jewish times, where precisely these two scenes are to be found above the Torah niche in the 3rd century synagogue of Dura Europos (now in the museum of Damascus). Nevertheless their presence in the Sinai church has two other implications. One is typological, whereby an Old Testament scene prefigures one from the New. Just as the Moses scenes mean an epiphany so does the Transfiguration, with the difference, however, that in the former Moses was not allowed to see the Lord, while in the latter the three disciples saw with their own eyes the transformation from the human to the divine nature of Christ. Secondly, there is the topographical aspect. After all, behind the apse lies the chapel of the Burning Bush, and looking out of the window, one sees the Djebel Musa, the steep mountain, where according to monastic tradition the Receiving of the Law took place.

The mosaicist who laid out and designed the program was a great

85

artist, and we believe that he must have come from Constantinople. In a very sovereign manner he used different modes of expression: rather abstract features for Christ, stressing in this manner the Divine, and more naturalistic ones for the Prophets, very calm in the case of Moses and highly emotional in that of Elijah. This juxtaposition is repeated in the faces of the tranquil John and the soulful James and once more in those of the tragic John the Baptist and the divine Virgin. Compared with the almost contemporary mosaics of S. Vitale and S. Apollinare in Classe in Ravenna, the Sinai mosaic has a more painterly quality in the tradition of the Hellenistic Greek East, while the Ravennate are more linear with stress on a higher degree of physical reality, being in this respect closer to the Roman than the Byzantine tradition.

There is no doubt that the chief master of the Sinai mosaic worked with apprentices of lesser quality, for side by side with his magnificent executions can be seen work of much weaker hands, but the general layout shows perfect unity and great artistic skill. Most remarkable is the fact that the mosaic is in mint condition and has never been restored. Never again did Sinai have such a brilliant period as during the time of Justinian, its generous founder.

This soon became apparent when — about a century later and most likely after the Muslim occupation — the monks decided to expand the program of the apse. Whether there was no more space for mosaic decoration or whether mosaicists were no longer available, two paintings in the unusual encaustic technique on the marble revetment were added to the pilasters framing the apse. To the left the Sacrifice of Isaac is depicted as taking place on an altar with an altar cloth — a clear hint that this scene was meant to be and was surely generally understood as a prefiguration of Christ's sacrificial death. The pilaster to the right, in front of which stands St. Catherine's tomb, was covered by an icon of the title saint in a rococo marble frame. I reasoned that underneath there should be

169

a companion-piece to Isaac's Sacrifice, i.e. another 7th century encaustic panel. In 1963, after having obtained permission from the late archbishop, the venerable and understanding Porphyrios III, to remove the frame, indeed another encaustic panel did come to light, depicting, as confirmed by the inscription, the Sacrifice of Jephthah's daughter. This scene, unique in Early Christian monumental art, depicts the soldier Jephthah, who had made the vow that, if victorious, he would sacrifice whatsoever would come out of the door of his house (Jud. XI, 30 ff.). Fate was unkind — it was his own daughter and, true to his vow he sacrificed his only child. This event is depicted here in a most gruesome manner, the victim's throat being cut by a sword. It is clear from the writings of some Syrian church fathers that this scene must be understood as a prefiguration of Christ's sacrifice. Artistically these two encaustic panels, of a lesser quality than the mosaic proper, were in all probability executed by an icon painter who came from Palestine, most likely Jerusalem.

Once more the mosaic technique was used, though on a more modest scale. At a certain time — we do not know exactly when — the open court which enclosed the most holy site, i.e. the Burning Bush, was turned into a chapel. A commemorative marble plaque covers the very location of the bush and an altar was erected over it; standing in a small apse whose conch was embellished by a simple mosaic. It shows merely a cross in a circle and an inscription which names an archbishop Solomon, but whose date, presumably from the early 11th century, was erased.

Fresco painting played a comparatively minor role, compared with the normal orthodox church interior. From the period of the great apse mosaic we have only the decoration of a tiny chapel carved out of the thickness of the southwest wall. The side walls are covered by an imitation of marble encrustation in the pure classical tradition and the tunnel vault is coffered in the ancient manner; the panels with birds and rosettes being divided by 11, 12 garlands. A jewel-studded cross painted in the niche at the east end is the only indication that we are dealing with a Christian chapel.

Only a few but characteristic examples of fresco painting have survived and they are from two flourishing periods of later centuries. After the fall of Constantinople in 1453 St. Catherine's must have profited from an influx of refugee artists. In the second half of the 15th century the chapel of St. James to the left of the chapel of the Burning Bush received an apse decoration which has in the center the Virgin of the Burning Bush, flanked by James and John Chrysostom on the one side, and by Basil and — most fittingly — by Moses on the other. Christ in heaven above hands out a Gospelbook and a Tablet of the Law to the figures below. The same workshop filled a niche within the wall, which originally was part of a chapel, with a fresco of the Virgin with Child. What is remarkable is that these frescoes copy 12–13th century models with such faithfulness that at first sight one might be misled in attributing them (wrongly) to these centuries. About a century later the local school was firmly replaced by Cretan masters who excelled in the 16th and 17th century both as fresco and icon painters. But while Cretan icons on Sinai are extremely numerous, the activity of fresco painters was limited to a Last Judgment which covers the east wall of the Refectory and is dated 1573.

168

With the exception of the apse mosaic, the greatest artistic treasure of Sinai is the collection of icons. It is a collection that is outstanding and unique in several respects. First the sheer number of icons is astounding. I made my own checklist and counted precisely 2044. This list comprises not only the icons which are in the church and the various chapels within the monastery, but also those hidden in the chapels of the neighboring valleys and mountain peaks all around. The monks realized that the icons in the outlying chapels, very rarely visited by the monks, were endangered and I was authorized to bring all those which I considered to be of artistic value into the monastery. Most of them went into the storeroom which once had housed the old Library and whose shelves had been emptied after the transfer of the books into the new concrete building erected between the two world wars. When we first visited this storeroom it had more than 600 icons. But then the monks became concerned about the safety of the icons in the side chapels of the basilica and transferred most of them also into the storeroom. Consequently the storeroom now houses more than a thousand. A selection of the very best icons is now exhibited in a special room labelled "Picture Gallery" next to the new library. This clearly reveals the thinking of the present-day monks who realize that the great mass of visitors are no longer pilgrims who come for the veneration of the icons, but tourists who are interested in them as works of art.

Yet in the church proper the icons still serve their original function. The focal point is the iconostasis which traditionally has two icons at either side of the Royal Doors, three of the four forming the so-called Deesis, i.e. Christ between the Virgin and John the Baptist as intercessors. The fourth icon is usually reserved for the title saint of the church, in this case St. Catherine, dressed in imperial robes, wearing a crown and surrounded with the paraphernalia of her martyrdom, i.e. the wheel, and the instruments which allude to her learnedness. Jeremias of Crete painted these icons in 1612. Where, in earlier instances, the beam over the architrave contained representations of the twelve great feasts, by the 17th century this cycle was enlarged by additional scenes from the Passion and distributed over individual panels. During the liturgy the priest burns incense and reads the Prayer of Intercession before the icons of the iconostasis. Moreover within the nave stands a lectern surmounted by a baldachin the so-called proskynetarion. Here the icon of the day is displayed, in front of which the priest bows deeply (therefore the term "proskynetarion"), and kisses the icon before he enters the sanctuary in the so-called "Little Introitus". These icons of the day hang in long rows on the North and South walls of the aisles of the church in the order of the calendar, so that when one is brought back the one next to it is taken from

89

the hook and taken to the proskynetarion. Large-size icons hang on the walls which, because of their size, cannot be moved and still others are placed on pedestals to be in closer contact with the worshipper. But even the greatest icon collection does not have an icon of every saint. To take care of this need the calendar icons were invented whereby all the saints distributed over several panels were lined up in long rows. In the church a set of twelve such icons, one for each month, are hung on the twelve columns and a candle is lighted in front of the icon which includes the saint of the day. So, in spite of the fact that a large number of icons have been withdrawn from their original function and exhibited in museum fashion, a sufficient number are still involved in the celebration of the liturgy.

80–83

The collection is unique in that from the 6th century on, i.e. not long after icons were invented and soon thereafter introduced into the service of the church, every century is represented right down to modern times. In 1958 I attended the funeral of Pater Pachomios, the last icon and fresco painter at Sinai, and with his death the uninterrupted tradition of icon painting in the monastery came to an end. Pachomios was held in the highest esteem as one of the most saintly of monks. Yet while his icons, thoroughly westernized in style, would not find much appreciation among art lovers today, he merits recognition for his deep concern about the preservation of the icons in the monastery. It was he who, because of the venerability of any icon, collected every fragment he could find and saved it, and art historians owe him a great debt for the work he did in preservation and conservation.

The Sinai collection has increased our knowledge of icon painting beyond our expectations, and yet it has raised more problems than scholarship has so far been able to solve. One important point becomes quite clear from the outset: that the collection does not represent a cross-section of icon painting as a whole, but that it was brought together under very special circumstances that were tied to the history of the monastery.

90

Clearly the desert is not conducive to the creation of a refined, distinctive style of its own and the icons the monastery possesses were either brought as gifts or produced by artists who had been trained in other places and then settled at Sinai. In many instances it is difficult to decide between these two circumstances but the following considerations may shed some light on this problem: when one deals with isolated icons the likelihood is that they were brought as gifts, but when one finds a whole series of icons by the same hand or by the same workshop, it is more probable that they were produced in the monastery. Furthermore, in the case of the iconostasis beams, which had to be made to order with precise measurements, it is once more most likely that they were produced on the spot.

Moreover many icons were made, if not in the monastery itself, at least *for* the monastery. Iconographically they relate to the Holy Sites of Sinai, concentrating in the main on three subjects: (1) the Virgin of the Burning Bush to whom the monastery was originally dedicated; (2) Moses either loosening his sandals, referring to the spot on which the monastery was built, or receiving the tablets, referring to the top of the Moses mountain; and (3) St. Catherine, to whom the monastery was rededicated in the 10th or 11th century. Finally we must take into consideration that at different times colonies of Syrian, Georgian, Latin and later Slavic monks lived in the monastery; all of whom were in need of icons for their own chapels. These various factors contributed to the highly diversified character of the Sinai collection.

The rich period of icon painting under Justinian and his immediate successors, has made Sinai the only place in the world which has preserved a substantial number of first-rate icons executed in the encaustic technique, i.e. wax painting. It may be mentioned in passing that three more, preserved today in the museum of Kiev, actually come from Sinai. Among these early icons are three great masterpieces which, ever since they became known rather recently, entered almost every handbook on Byzantine art. Because of their high quality it has been generally assumed that they are imports from Constantinople, possibly even imperial gifts.

52, 54 One represents the nearly life-size bust of Christ Pantocrator, blessing and holding a jewel-studded Gospel book. The hieratic frontality and the impression of aloofness on the one hand and the avoidance of strict symmetry and the enlivenment of the face achieved by different arching of the eyebrows on the other, strike a harmony between the divine and the human nature of Christ. The second masterpiece depicts the Virgin

77 enthroned between the Saints Theodore and George who flank her like pylons while two angels look up at the hand of God. The extraordinary coloristic expressiveness of this painter may be seen in the distinction between the head of the aloof Virgin with the olive-colored shading of the eyes and the more realistic faces of the soldier saints, one sunburned and the other pallid, while the heads of the ethereal angels are rendered in a more impressionistic manner. The third masterpiece represents an almost

89 life-size bust of Saint Peter. His penetrating look is that of a spiritual leader rather than a simple fisherman, full of tension and pent-up energy, qualities also expressed in the swirl of the hair and the very marked criss-crossing highlights of his garment.

With the conquest of Sinai and Egypt by Islam in 640 the ties with Constantinople were severed for some time and the icons from the 7–9th and well into the 10th century show a style in which the classical heritage recedes in favor of a rougher and more abstract style. Its center, as far as icon production is concerned, was apparently Palestine and Jerusalem in particular, with whose patriarchate Sinai is closely connected to the present day. This period coincides with that of iconoclasm (726–843 A.D.) in the Byzantine empire proper in which the production of icons was banned by imperial decrees. With Palestine being out of reach of these decrees, the icon production continued there and once more we have a

92

period of which only Sinai has preserved icons in considerable numbers. The two encaustic paintings on the marble revetments with the Sacrifices of Isaac and Jephthah's daughter, already mentioned, are most characteristic examples of this Palestinian icon style in its early phase. i.e. the 7th century, while an Ascension of Christ which forms the center of a triptych is a characteristic example of its late phase. The painterly style of the classical tradition had given way to a hard graphic style whose effect is not dissimilar to early woodcuts of the 15th century, and like them maintained a highly decorative quality. The Virgin of this Ascension stands in front of a bush with red flowers which may well suggest flames and allude to the Burning Bush and this in turn suggests that the icon may have been made if not *in,* at least *for* the Sinai monastery.

In what we call the Middle Byzantine period, from the end of iconoclasm until the conquest of Constantinople by the Venetians (843–1204 A.D.), Sinai was open again to influences from the capital. There are imports of great quality, as well as works of art executed by artists trained in the style of the capital which in these centuries lived through a second golden age and became in all matters of art and culture the arbiter in the orthodox world. The delicate and refined style of the end of this period, i.e. the 12th century, may be seen in the fascinating icon of the Heavenly Ladder of John Climacus, who at the end of the 6th century was abbot of Sinai and wrote a most popular monastic treatise on how to reach heaven by climbing 30 rungs of a ladder — standing, for the number of virtues the monks must acquire to achieve their goal. Temptations cause many of them to fall, dramatically pictorialized by devils who pull them from the ladder. But John Climacus himself is the first to reach heaven, as does his immediate follower, another abbot of Sinai. This icon which strikingly reveals the spirit of Eastern monasticism may well have been executed in the monastery itself by an artist trained in the Constantinopolitan tradition.

169

74

117

116

93

In the 13th century the impact of the Crusades was strongly felt in the monastery. Pilgrims from the West brought great wealth and gifts and the monastery, officially under the jurisdiction of the Latin Patriarch in Jerusalem, respectively the suffragan bishop of Petra, had one of its most flourishing periods. Greek and Latin artists were active at the same time and great projects were commissioned. The already-mentioned twelve great calendar icons hung up on the columns were painted at this time. So were a group of huge icons in which the central figure of a saint is surrounded on the frame by scenes from his life — scenes which were inspired by illustrated Saint's Lives. These works were apparently destined to be the key icons in the chapels of the respective saints. The icon of St. Catherine, standing frontally, dressed in imperial garments and wearing a high crown must originally have been close to her tomb. Most likely it stood in the place which is now occupied by a huge 19th century icon of St. Catherine under a heavy gold cover, a so-called riza, while the original icon is now displayed in the gallery. The gallery also has a huge icon of a half figure of St. Nicholas, surrounded with scenes from his life, an icon which originally was made for a chapel dedicated to this church father but which no longer exists. To the same set belong two equally large icons of John the Baptist and Saint George, likewise taken out of their respective chapels and found in the gallery, while only one such icon, that of Saint Panteleimon, surrounded by scenes of his life, is still to be seen in its original context at the entrance to the chapel within the basilica dedicated to this physician saint.

One of the greatest surprises in studying the collection was the discovery of a great number of icons which were obviously executed by Crusader artists from various nations. While there is one icon done apparently by an English artist and another presumably by a German, the vast majority were executed by Italian painters from all parts of the country, the heavily Greek-influenced South, from Tuscany, and especially from Venice which seems to have played the greatest role. But there are also icons by French painters from the period when Saint Louis resided in Palestine from 1250–1254. After the fall of Jerusalem in 1244, the most flourishing center was Acre from where the artists came who worked at Sinai, because there can be no doubt, for various reasons, that a great number of Crusader icons were actually painted in the monastery. An Italian artist, e.g., executed an iconostasis beam which shows the Deesis in the center, Christ flanked by the Virgin and John the Baptist, six Apostles, three at either side, and by the soldier saints George and Procopius. The style of these figures of three-quarter size, placed under gothic pointed arches, suggests Tuscany as the place of origin though the precise center needs still to be determined. With a greater sense for physical reality, the Italian painter, in spite of his attempt to imitate a Greek model, reveals his Western provenance. What is remarkable is the fact that the Western artist accepts from the Eastern rite the iconostasis beam and this suggests that the Latins who had their own chapel in the monastery called "St. Catherine of the Franks" — it no longer exists — apparently decorated it in the orthodox fashion. We believe an icon with a Moses bust to have been made by the hand of a French artist. This bust shows the prophet with a soulful look — an emotional quality quite different from the one achieved by Byzantine artists of this time who depicted their saints aloof even when they tried to show expressive faces.

After the Crusaders had left, the monastery reestablished its close connection with Constantinople and from the so-called Palaeologan period (1261–1453) it owns a series of very refined icons in the style of the capital, representing the later and somewhat mannered phase of Byzantine painting. From this period onwards, the Sinai collection lost its position of uniqueness in the history of icon painting. Beginning with the 14th century, equally good icons were made in Greece, the Balkans and in various parts of the Near East.

Apparently it was only after the fall of Constantinople, in 1453, that the monastery again became an active place of icon and — as we have already mentioned — even of fresco painting. There is an obvious eagerness to preserve the Byzantine tradition whose very existence seemed to have been threatened and the main aim of the artists was — just as in the case of the frescoes — to imitate as closely as possible models of the 12th–13th centuries when the monastery had had a flourishing period. Huge iconostasis icons with Christ, the Virgin, John the Baptist and equally large ones of archangels and Apostles were copied and, if it were not for a slightly softer modelling of the flesh and a greenish background instead of gold, one would often be in doubt as to whether one is dealing with a 15th or a 13th century icon. Among the icons copied again and again were those depicting the Last Judgment. The monastery has two beautiful ones of the 12th century in the style of the capital and they became the models for several copies in the 16th century which made no alterations in the iconography, and betray their later date only by slight stylistic changes.

102, 104

But soon the monastery's own production was superseded by that of Cretan painters. Crete had become the very center of Greek icon painters and their products were exported to the entire orthodox world. In spite of the fact that much has become known of Cretan icon painting within the last decades, the extraordinarily rich collection of Cretan icons at Sinai will greatly enrich our knowledge. We have already mentioned that Jeremias was responsible for the icons in the huge iconostasis. Moreover there are outstanding individual icons, quite a number of which are signed by well-known painters such as Michael Damaskenos, Angelos, Klotzas, Lambardos, Demetrios, Victor, Tzanes and still others. There are others, which are not signed which are of equal quality.

One has always to be reminded that Sinai was open to Christianity at large and that at different times colonies of monks from other Christian

96

continued on page 153

54

52, 54 Encaustic icon of Christ Pantocrator. 84 × 45,5 cm. One of the oldest and best kept icons of the monastery. The icon is probably from Constantinople. For a long time it was dated to the thirteenth century because it had been almost completely painted over. In fact, it dates back to the sixth century.

52 Detail of 54.

53 A view of the old library. A great number of icons, which could not be stored in the church in the side chapels because of lack of space, used to be kept here. The monastery possesses more than 2,000 icons, from the sixth century to contemporary times.

55 The Prophet Eli-
jah. Around 1200.
130×67 cm.

56 Detail of 55.

57 Deesis and the
Holy Fathers of Sinai.
13th century.
57.3×42.5 cm.

55

58

60

58 Icon with Virgin
Glykophilousa. Cre-
tan. 16th century.
44.1×35.6 cm.

59 Virgin Glykophi-
lousa. 13th–14th cen-
tury. 24.9×18.6 cm.

60 Virgin with the im-
plements of the Pas-
sion. Cretan. 16th cen-
tury. 25.4×20.2 cm.

61 Virgin Glykophi-
lousa. Cretan.
16th–17th century.
25.2×18.8 cm.

62 Virgin with Child
and John the Evangel-
ist. 16th–17th century.
22.6×17.7 cm.

63 Virgin Hodegetria.
Popular style of uncer-
tain date. 25.4×18 cm.

64 The Forty Martyrs
of Sebaste. Uncertain
date. 38.3×28.9 cm.

59

61

63

62

65

67

66

68

69

70

65 Angel from the Annunciation. Constantinople. End of 12th century. 61 × 42 cm.

66 Archangel Michael. Popular style. Uncertain date. 31.4 × 20 cm.

67 The Miracle at Chone. The archangel Michael saves the hut of the monk Archippus. Constantinople, First half of 12th century. 37.5 × 30.7 cm.

68 Saint Theodosia. 15th century (?). 21.7 × 14 cm.

69 Bust of archangel Gabriel. Sinaitic work about 15th–16th century. 33.6 × 25.9 cm.

70 Saint Catherine with scenes from her life in the frame. Sinaitic work. 75.2 × 51.1 cm.

71 Head of Saint George. 14th century. 36 × 28.5 cm.

72 Sea shell. Moses loosening the sandals before the Virgin in the Burning Bush. Sinaitic work. Modern. 22 × 19 cm.

72

74

74 Ascension of Christ. Center of a triptych. Sinaitic work under Palestinian influence. 9th–10th century. 41.8 × 27.1 cm.

75 The Virgin of the Burning Bush surrounded by Moses, Aaron, Elijah and Saint Catherine. Sinaitic work. 17th century. 26.6 × 21.1 cm.

76 Saint Sergius before the Virgin with Peter and John. Russian. 17th century. 30 × 24.3 cm.

77 Encaustic icon. Virgin with Child between the soldier saints Theodor and George. Constantinople. 2nd half of 6th century. 68.5 × 49.7 cm.

75

73

73 John the Baptist. Icon in the iconostasis of the chapel of the Holy Fathers. Cretan school. Early 17th century. 105.7 × 66 cm.

76

77

78 Saint David of Thessalonike preaches from an almond tree. Called the "New David" he is here depicted together with King David. Cretan school. 16th century. 20.8 × 17.2 cm.

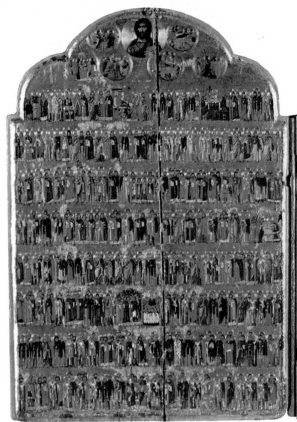

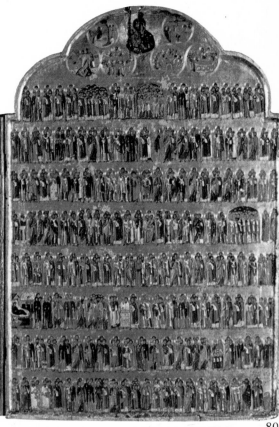

80

79 The Birth of the
Virgin. Detail from 80.

80 Diptych with the
full calendar of the
twelve months. Con-
stantinople. 12th cen-
tury. Each wing
36.5 × 24.6 cm.

81, 82, 83 The Forty
Martyrs of Sebaste.
Altogether there are
more than 1,200
figures ranging from
2.5 to 3 cm in height.
In spite of their small
size the artist suc-
ceeded in lending each
figure its own personal
bearing and features.
One can only be aston-
ished at these marvel-
lous works of art, espe-
cially when taking into
account that their
heads are only approx.
3 mm large. Details
from 80.

81

82

84

85

86

87

84 Bust of Saint Ananias. Cretan school. 16th–17th century. 24.1 × 19 cm.

85 Bust of Saint Nicholas. Russian. 17th century. 18.5 × 14.1 cm.

86 Wing of a triptych. Busts of Saint Charitonos and Saint Theodosios. Palestinian school. 8th–9th century. 22.2 × 9.4 cm.

87 Bust of John Climacus, author of the Scala Paradisi. Sinaitic work. 15th century. 23.2 × 18.8 cm.

88 Encaustic icon. Enthroned Christ in the manifestations of the Ancient of Days, Pantocrator and Immanuel. About 7th century. 76 × 53.5 cm.

89 Encaustic icon.
Saint Peter. Above
medallions of Christ
between John the
Evangelist (?) and the
Virgin. Constantino-
ple. End of 6th–
early 7th century.
92.5 × 53.1 cm.

90

91

90 Crucifixion. Work
of a Crusader artist.
13th century.
35.3 × 25.3 cm.

91 Saint Alexius.
Russian. 17th–18th
century. 31 × 27.3 cm.

92 Iconostasis beam. Work of an Italian Crusader artist, made at Sinai, probably for the chapel of St. Catherine of the Franks. The Central Deesis is flanked behind the Virgin by Peter (left) and John the Baptist (right). Middle of 13th century. 43 × 168.8 cm

93 Bust of Saint Nicholas. On frame 16 scenes from his life. Sinaitic work. First half of 13th century. 82 × 56.9 cm.

95 Bust of Christ Pantocrator. 13th century. 20.2 × 15.4 cm.

96 Detail from an icon. Typical hand position which often occurs on icons of Christ or saints.

97 Bust of Saint Antipas. Probably by a Venetian Crusader artist; made at Sinai. 2nd half 13th century. 58.2 × 44.9 cm.

95

93

94

94 Icon in the iconostasis of St. George's chapel. Christ Pantocrator. Sinaitic work. 2nd half 15th century. 97 × 63.5 cm.

96

98

99

100

101

102

101 Dog-headed Saint Christophoros. 17th-18th century. 39 × 27.5 cm.

102 Detail of a Last Judgment. Constantinople. Middle 12th century. Total icon 62.2 × 45.8 cm.

103 Ascension of Elijah. Sinaitic work. Second half 15th century. 36.4 × 28 cm.

98 Saint George on horseback. Sinaitic work. Second half of 15th century. 39.8 × 25.8 cm.

99 Saints Sergius and Bacchus on horseback. Crusader artist; made at Sinai. 13th century. This is the back of a bilateral icon whose front shows a bust of the Virgin Hodegetria. 95.2 × 62.7 cm.

100 The three Cappadocian church fathers Basil, John Chrysostom and Gregory of Nazianzus. Cretan school. 15th–16th century. 37.6 × 32.1 cm.

104 Detail of a Last Judgment. Constantinople. End 11th-early 12th century. Total icon 48 × 35.5 cm.

105 Detail of a Last Judgment. Crusader icon made at Sinai. 13th century. Total icon 39.5 × 32.4 cm.

106 Last Judgment. Sinaitic work. Second half 15th century. 28.5 × 21.2 cm.

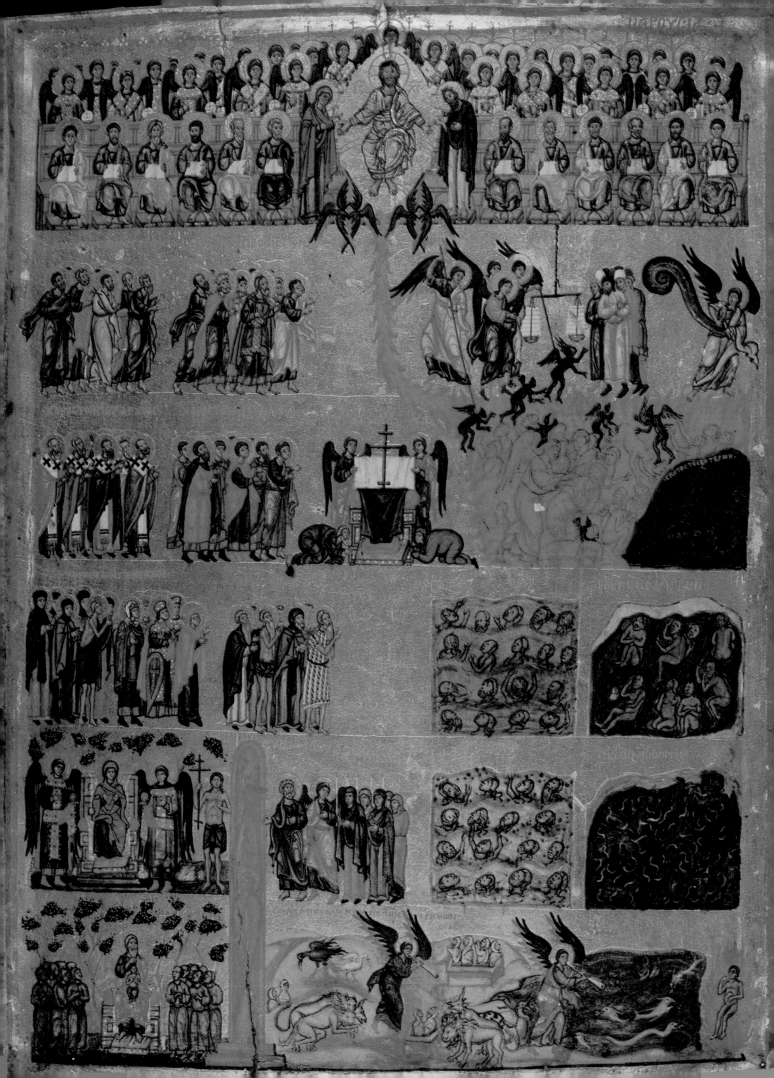

107

109

110

108

111

107–114 Views of the monastery from the 18th and 19th century

ΕΚ ΒΑΘΡΩΝ ΑΝΗΓΕΡΘ Ω̄ ΙΕΡΑ ΤΩ̄ ΜΟΝΑΣΤΗΡΙΟΝ ΤΩ̄ ΣΙΝΑΪ̈Ϲ ΟΡΟΥϹ. ΕΝΘΑ ΕΛΑΛΗϹΕΝ Ο ΘΕΟϹ Τᾱ ΜΩΥΣΗ. ΠΑΡΑ ΤΩ̄ ΤΑΠΕΙΝΩ̄ ΒΑΣΙΛΕΩϹ ΡΩΜΑΙΩΝ ΙΟΥΣΤΙΝΙΑΝΟΥ ΠΡΟΣ ΑΙΔΙΟΝ ΜΝΗΜΟΣΥΝΟΝ ΑῩΤ̄

ΚΑΙ Τ̄Ϲ ΣΥΖΥΓΟῩ ΘΕΟΔΩΡΑΣ. ΕΛΑΒΕ ΤΕΛΟΣ. ΜΕΤΑ Τᾱ ΤΡΙΑΚΟΣΤΩ̄ ΕΤΕ̄Ϲ ΤῈ̄Ϲ ΒΑΣΙΛΕΙΑΣ Τ̄. ΚΑΙ ΚΑΤΕΣΤΗϹΕΝ ΕΝ ΑῩΤ̄. ΗΓΟΥΜΕΝΟΝ. ΟΝΟΜΑΤΙ ΔΟΥΛΑΝ. ΕΙΚΕΙ ΤΡΙΗΚΙΑΣ ΕΚΑ ΑΙΔΕΧ̄Υ

114

115

116

115 Library cod. arab. 343 (A. D. 1612). The Heavenly Ladder of John Climacus. Fol. 13 v. Monks ascending and falling from ladder.

116 The cave in which John Climacus lived is some two hours journey away from the monastery. He died here in the first half of the seventh century.

117 Icon of the Heavenly Ladder. Perhaps painted at Sinai. Second half of the 12th century. 41×21.6 cm.

118

118 Mosaic icon of Saint Demetrius. Constantinople. 13th century. 19 × 14.6 cm.

119 Apse mosaic with Transfiguration of Christ. 6th century. On the triumphal arch the Lamb of God with the medallions of John the Baptist and the Virgin and two archangels (= the earliest Deesis) in the window zone the two Moses scenes. In the apse: Christ (center), the prophet Elijah (far left), Moses (far right). The Apostles John und James are seen kneeling. The recumbent Peter (below center) on the ground. The medaillons show the 12 Apostles, 16 prophets, King David and two sponsors of the mosaics.

121

122

120 Detail of an apse mosaic: The central figure of Christ symbolizing the twin nature of Christ: divine and yet of man.

121–125 Details from the apse mosaic.

121 Mosaic. Prophet Elijah at Christ's left.
122 Prophet Moses.
123 The Lamb of God.
124 Saint James.
125 Saint Peter.

123

124

125

126

127

126–128 Details from the apse mosaic.

126 Moses receiving the tablet of the law in the shape of a scroll.

127 Moses before the burning bush.

128 Head of Moses.

129

131

130

132

129–136 Details from
the apse mosaic.
6th century.

129 John the Deacon.
130 Ezekiel.
131 Daniel.
132 Malachi.
133 Haggai.
134 Jeremiah.
135 Zephaniah.
136 Longinus, the abbot.

133

138

137 Beautifully en-
graved silver oil lamps
emit their soft light day
and night above the
tomb of Saint
Catherine.

138 Detail of one of
the large candelabras.

139 Encolpion with
cameo of Saint Cath-
erine framed with
enamel and pearls.
Russian. 17th century.

139

140 Silver and gold chalice with enamels. Made, as indicated by inscriptions in Greek and Latin at the bottom, as a gift of Charles VI, King of France, to the Church of St. Catherine on Mount Sinai in 1411.

141 Bronze aquamanile in the shape of a dove. Islamic of the Fatimidic period (10th–12th century).

142

143

142–147 Painted
ceiling panels. About
13th–14th century.

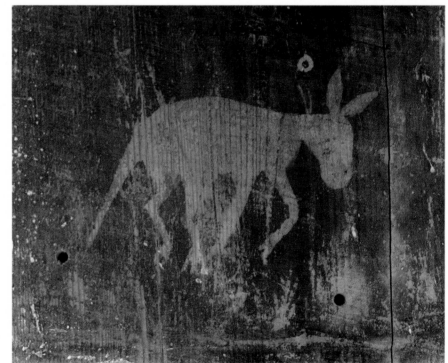

147

148 Library cod. gr. 339 (middle of 12th century). Gregory of Nazianzus. Homilies. Initials with various quadrupeds and birds.

149 Library cod. gr. 213 (A. D. 967). Lectionary of Mt. Horeb. Fol. 196 v. Beginning of the Passion readings.

ΕΥΑΓΓΕ ΛΙΑC ΥΝΟΙΝ

Τ ΠΑ Θ ΥC Τ ΚΥ
Κ Θ ΥΝΙΩΝ
ΙΥ ΧΥ

ΚΑ Ι Ω

ΙΠΕΝ
Ο ΚΣ
ΤΟΙC
ΕΑΥΤΟ
ΜΑΘΗΤΑΙC

ΝΥΝΕΔΟΞΑ
CΘΗΟΥCΤΟΥ
ΑΝΟΥ ; ΚΑΙ
Ο ΘΕΕΔΟΞΑ
CΘΗΕΝΑΥΤΩ
ΕΙΟΘΕΕΔΟΞΑ
CΘΗΕΝΑΥΤΩ.
ΚΑΙΟΘΕCΔΟ
ΞΑCΗΑΥΤΟΝ
ΕΝΑΥΤΩ ;
ΚΑΙΕΥΘΥC
ΔΟΞΑCΕΙΑΥ
ΤΟΝ ΤΕ
ΚΝΙΑ: ΕΤΙ
ΜΙΚΡΟΝ ΜΕ
ΘΥΜΩΝΗ
ΜΙ; ΖΗΤΗ
CΕΤΕΜΕ
ΚΑΙΚΑΘΩC

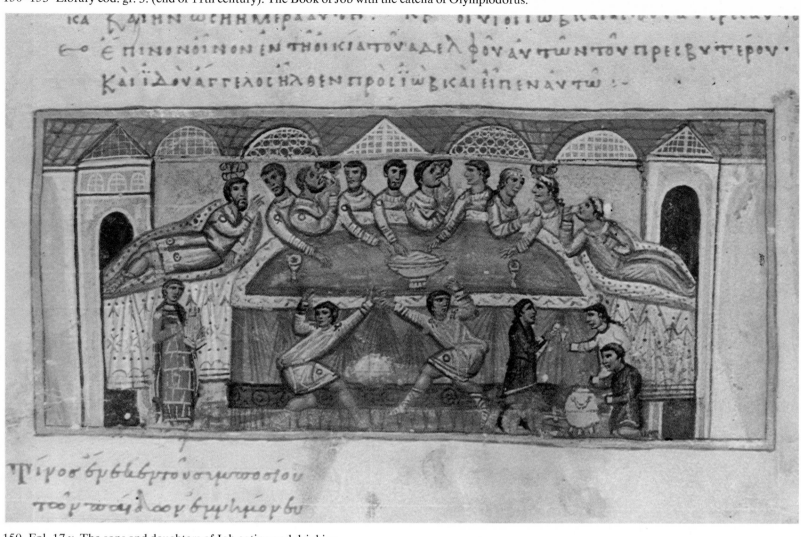

150 Fol. 17 v. The sons and daughters of Job eating and drinking.

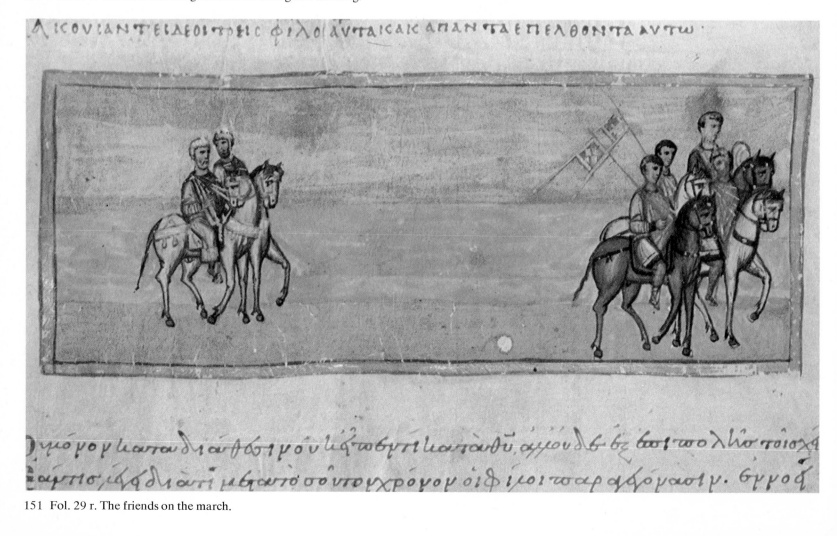

151 Fol. 29 r. The friends on the march.

152 Fol. 19 v. The Chaldaeans carry away the camels and slay the servants.

ΚΑΙ ΠΑΡΕΓΕΝΟΝΤΟ ΠΡΟΣ ΑΥΤΟΝ ΟΜΟΘΥΜΑΔΟΝ · ΝΟΜΑΟ ΕΝΑΜΑ

Μ Ιωσ ο νσο δε ρε ζε ζας τος ισον παραμυθια τον φιλον ησ παρουσια · αμα

153 Fol. 29 v. The friends on the march.

✝ ΤΟΥ ΑΥΤΟΥ. ΠΕΡΙ ΦΙΛΟΠΤΩΧΙΑC ✝

ἀδελφοὶ
καὶ σύντροφοι
τοῦ πτωχοῦ ἀδ
ἀπ᾽ αὐτῶν καὶ
τῆς θείας χά
ριτος τῶν δεῖς·
καὶ ἄλλος ἄλ
λου προσάγειν

δοκιμαζε[..]οισ
μέτροις μέτρου
μβρος δοξαζ θ
τὸν προῖ φιλο
πτωχίας λόγο·
μὴ τὸ μὴ χείρος·
ἀλλὰ φιλοτί
μος· ἵνα μὴ

155

156

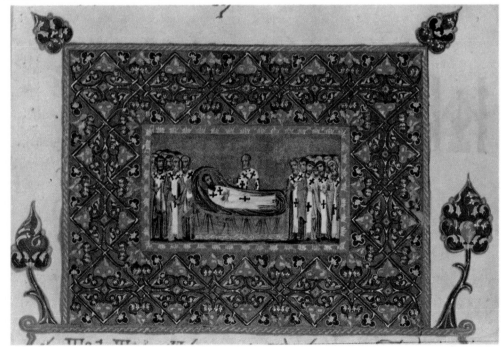

157

158

154 Library cod. gr. 339 (middle of 12th century). Gregory of Nazianzus. Fol. 341 v. Gregory preaching about the Love of the Poor.

155 Library cod. gr. 418 (12th century). John Climacus, the Heavenly Ladder. Fol. 279 r. Tranquillity.

156 Cod. gr. 418. Fol. 211 r. Discretion.

157 Headpiece of a 12th century lectionary.

158 Cod. gr. 339. Fol. 109 r. Homily on the Funeral of Saint Basil.

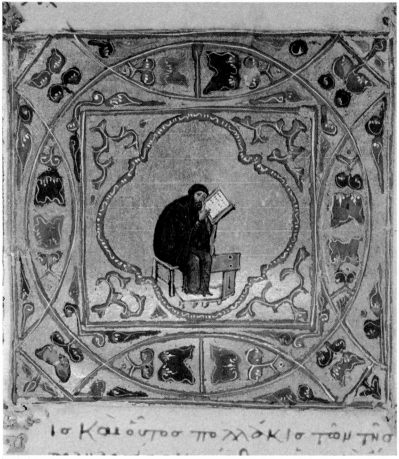

159

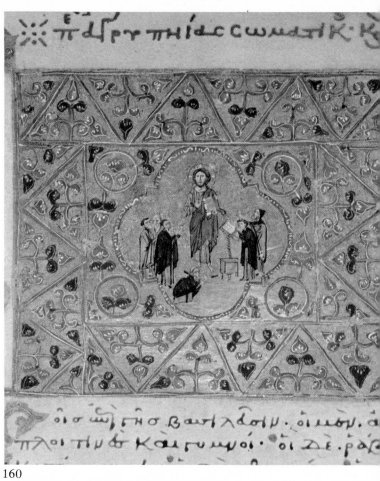

160

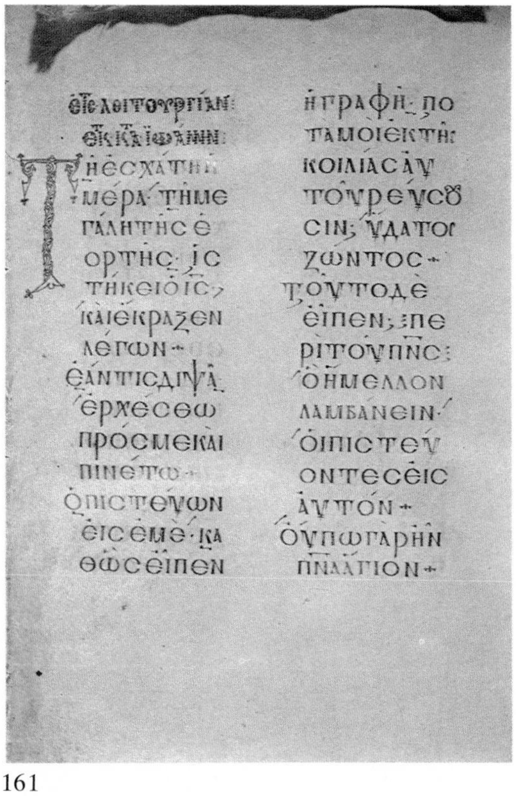

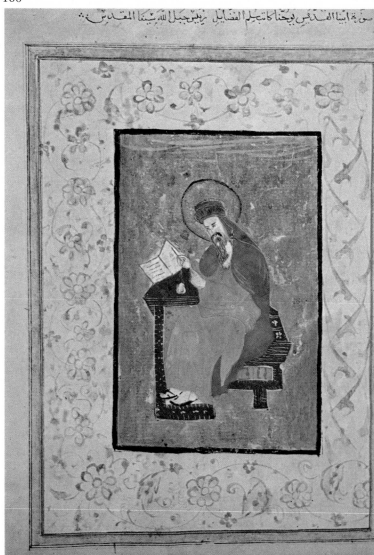

ἐκ λειτουργίαν
ἐκ κ(ατὰ) ἰωάννην
Τῇ ἐσχάτῃ ἡ
μέρᾳ τῇ με
γάλῃ τῆς ἑ
ορτῆς· ἱσ
τήκει ὁ ἰ(ησοῦ)ς
καὶ ἔκραζεν
λέγων·
ἐάν τις διψᾷ
ἐρχέσθω
πρός με καὶ
πινέτω·
ὁ πιστεύων
εἰς ἐμὲ· κα
θὼς εἶπεν
ἡ γραφή· πο
ταμοὶ ἐκ τῆς
κοιλίας αὐ
τοῦ ῥεύσου
σιν ὕδατος
ζῶντος·
τοῦτο δὲ
εἶπεν περὶ
τοῦ πν(εύματο)ς
ὃ ἤμελλον
λαμβάνειν
οἱ πιστεύ
οντες εἰς
αὐτόν·
οὔπω γὰρ ἦν
πν(εῦμ)α ἅγιον·

161

159 Library Cod. 418. John Climacus. Fol. 132 r. Sloth.

160 Cod. 418. Fol. 172 r. Wakefulness.

161 Page of an ancient manuscript.

162 Cod. arab. 343. (A. D. 1612). John Climacus. Fol. 3 r. The author writing.

163 Library Code. Fol. 4 v. Gregory of Nazianzus writing.

162

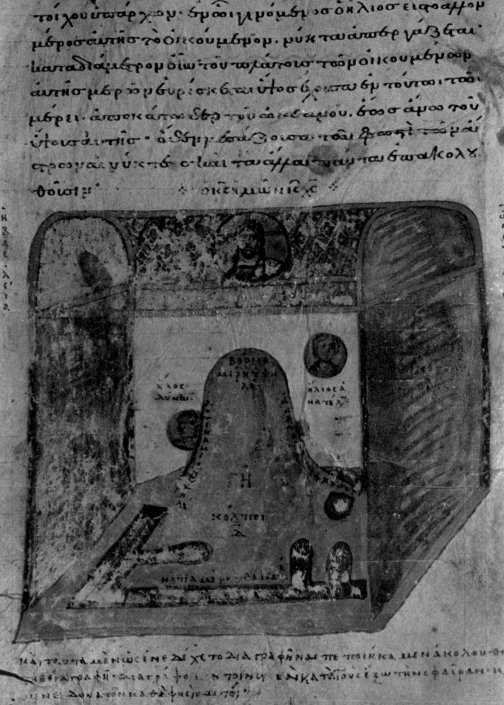

164

166

164–167 Library Cod. gr. 1186 (11th century). Cosmas Indicopleustes. Christian Topography.

164 Fol. 69 r. Scheme of the universe with the firmament in the shape of the ark of Noah.

165 Fol. 107 v. Ascension of Elijah.

166 Scheme of the universe.

167 Cod. gr. 1186. Fol. 86 v. The ark of the covenant and the twelve tribes of Israel.

165

τοῦ ραοῦ· τὸ ῥαμμον ματεῦναι αυτόμ· ὲωαμοοδε
αὐτοῦ. δυο χοροῦιὼμ δόζιω καταοκιαζομται τὸ
ἱλαατήριον· αὐτόομ τὸ ἱλαατήριον· τύπομ εἶναι
λάα τοῦ δ᾽ ωο τοιχι καταοαρκαὶ ὁ αποοτελοο· ὸμ
ωρὸ θθο ὁ θῶ ἱλαατήριον ὲμ τὼι αυτοῦ αἵματι·
ἡμαεῖ τωι· ὁκεῖμοο μὲμ τὸ ὲμ τλὶ ὸκ ιωλίι· ὲμαίμου
τὰμμοτριοοι παρεῖχι τλιὼ αφ δέρμ· οὐτοοδὲ ὲμ τωι
ἱ δίωοι αἵματι· ὁωοικ οατο τλιὼ αφ δέρμ τὼι κοομω·

φυλΗ ΔΑΝ ΒΘρΑς· φυλΗ ΜΕΜΙΩΝ· φυλΗ ΝΕΦΘΑΛΙ·

168 Refectory east wall. Fresco painting of the Last Judgment. Cretan school. 1573.

169 Encaustic painting on marble pilaster to the left of the apse. The Sacrifice of Isaac. 7th century.

churches resided in the monastery. Thus it is not surprising to find icons with Syriac and Arabic inscriptions representing a style which is different from the Greek and which has not yet been studied. There are icons with Georgian inscriptions. In one case they are calendar icons from the 11th century which are bilingual having a Georgian translation under the Greek inscriptions. The style is decidedly Greek and this means that the inscriptions do not necessarily decide the issue of the artist's nationality. Beginning with the 16th century there is an influx of Slavic, chiefly Russian, icons and sometimes the situation is the other way around: the inscriptions may be Greek, whereas the style is decidedly Russian. After Russia had assumed the role of the chief protector of all Orthodoxy it made large-scale supplies of altar implements, manuscripts and icons available to Greek monasteries. Along with Mt. Athos and Jerusalem, Sinai received a fair share of the often very sumptuous gifts. But as everywhere else in the Orthodox world, the increasingly strong influence of Western art, since the 18th century, has gradually destroyed the art of icon painting. The prevailing naturalism was incompatible with the spirituality of the world of icons. This was a world which depended on more abstract forms to convey the impression of the Divine and Otherworldliness.

Whereas the treasure of the icons has become appreciated only fairly recently, earlier visitors and scholars were mainly interested in the library which achieved world fame when, in the 1840s, Constantine Tischendorf discovered at Sinai one of the oldest and almost complete Bible manuscripts from the 4th century, generally known as the Codex Sinaiticus. There has been much written on the sensational circumstances of its finding and subsequent loan to Russia. The monastery counted on its return but Russia kept it and later paid a certain sum for it. After World War I it was sold to Great Britain and it now has come to rest in the British Library. Very recently, after a fire in the St. George's tower of the monastery, a walled-up room was discovered with more than 70 boxes of discarded fragments, mostly of very early manuscripts and papyri, including, it has been reported, eight more pages of the Sinaiticus.

This Bible manuscript proves that at the time of the monastery's founding books were given to it antedating the time of Justinian. Soon after the establishment of the monastery it must have started the production of its own manuscripts, mainly of liturgical books needed for the service. Thus it is hardly a surprise that a considerable number especially of New Testament and Psalter manuscripts have survived, written in a very early so-called uncial script. For these service books a much rougher parchment was used than for the manuscripts brought from the capital or other metropolitan centers, and they are quite worn from years of continuous handling.

The holdings of the library — in the same way as the collection of the icons — clearly reflect the growth and vicissitudes of the monastery built at the crossroad of many cultures. There were periods in which Syrian, Arabic, Georgian, Latin and Slavic monks lived at Sinai together with the Greek majority of monks many of whom had been raised under Moslem rule and probably spoke Arabic better than Greek. This explains the existence of bilingual prayer books in Greek and Arabic. Of the extant 148 ff. manuscripts more than two thousand are Greek, outnumbering all others. There are about seven hundred Arabic, all Christian texts, mostly liturgical and patristic. There are nearly three hundred Syriac manuscripts, about one hundred Georgian and forty Slavic. Surprisingly there is only one Latin manuscript, a 10th century Psalter which was wrongly classified as slavonicus 5. No doubt the Latins, when they were living in the monastery during the Crusader period, needed service books just as much as all the others. The loss of Latin manuscripts can only be explained by willful destruction, probably after the 16th century when the Slavic impact became very strong. The proof of this is the quantity of cut up Latin pages that were used to repair damaged books in other languages.

154

Where were the books originally housed? Since most of them were service books, it would seem most likely that they were kept close to the sanctuary where the service was conducted. At the east end of the south aisle there is an old — now unused — sacristy which is directly accessible from the presbytery and which has a second floor. Though it cannot be proved it seems quite likely that the books were stored here. Then, in 1734, when enlightenment had reached even this far corner of the world, a library, in the modern sense of the word, was built. Soon, when the influx of scholars began, this seems no longer to have sufficed and the library was moved to a double room next to the upper Panagia Chapel, where scholars had no direct access to the shelves and the books were handed out from behind a protective grille. Finally for reasons of safety and fire hazards a new spacious library was installed between 1930 and 1942 in the huge wing built of concrete which now occupies the whole southwest side of the monastery.

The first centuries after Moslem domination seem to have been difficult. The books produced between the 7th and 9th centuries and well into the 10th are very rough and adorned with only the simplest kind of ornament. In contrast a Gospel lectionary dated 967 A.D. and according to the colophon written on Mount Horeb, i.e. Sinai, is exuberantly decorated with ornaments which show the influence of the arabesque and of an orientalizing animal style which, as the design of a griffin clearly demonstrates, depends on Sassanian art. At the same time imported manuscripts arrived from Constantinople exemplifying the very best ever produced in Byzantine art. There is a Gospel lectionary from around the year 1000 with the text written page by page in golden uncials and with miniatures of the standing Christ, the Virgin, the four evangelists and a monk Peter of Monabata. These figures of the greatest refinement combine spiritual qualities, expressed by dematerialized bodies, with the classical heritage by mastering classical draperies and free movement — a

149

155

combination achieved only in Byzantium in her best periods. The most frequent miniatures are, of course, the portraits of the evangelists and the Sinai library has its fair share of them. In addition I should like to discuss, at least briefly, four outstanding manuscripts with larger cycles of miniatures.

Among the Old Testament manuscripts there is a luxurious codex which contains the book of Job with the lengthy catena by Olympiodoros added in the wide margins. Next to the Psalter, the Book of Job is the most often illustrated book of the Septuagint. Its contemplative content and literary excellence had a great appeal to the Orthodox world. The copy at Sinai from the end of the 11th century is different in style from all the other 150-153 Job manuscripts and may have been produced either in Constantinople or under Constantinopolitan influence. It is illustrated in a rather ascetic style which is a clear reaction to the classicizing style of the 10th century, i.e. the period of the Macedonian dynasty. The illustrators of the Book of Job were chiefly attracted by the first two chapters which narrate in great detail the vicissitudes of the great sufferer. We see the banquet of his children and their perishing, the suffering Job on the dung heap and the travels of the three friends who are going to join him in long conversations.

The most luxurious manuscript at Sinai is a collection of the sixteen 148, 154, 158, 163 liturgical homilies of Gregory of Nazianzus, written and illuminated in the middle of the 12th century at the imperial Pantocratoros monastery in Constantinople. In the title miniature the church father, dressed in somber monastic garb, writes his homilies within a rich setting which in a decorative way combines elements of outer architecture with marble 163 encrustation from church interiors. Each homily is preceded by a miniature representing either a Christological feast or the preaching Gregory or other scenes from his life, all of which are surrounded by wide frames of 154 the most luxurious ornamentation formed by flowers and rosettes interwoven in the most intricate patterns. And last but not least, the

156

illustrator displayed an inexhaustible imagination in the innumerable initials, formed of birds and quadrupeds in the most unusual positions in order to fit the form of the letters.

148

We have previously discussed the icon with the Heavenly Ladder of John Climacus which is based on an illustration of the edifying treatise known under this title. Likewise from the 12th century the Sinai library owns a manuscript which in addition to the ladder picture possesses one illustration to each of the 30 chapters which correspond to the rungs of the ladder. Here we see the monks in pursuit of virtues as well as being victims of temptations and in this way we get an insight into the monks' thoughts and lives: how they pray, how they worship icons, their concern about writing books by lamplight and so on. Like the figures of the Job manuscript the monks are depicted in very small scale with almost weightless bodies, set against a gold ground as if they were already removed from this world. And as in the Gregory manuscript each miniature is surrounded by a broad frame, ornamented with a flower petal motif of great variety and delicacy. The popularity of this iconastic treatise on Sinai is indicated by a 17th century Arabic copy written by Thabit, a Christian monk from Hama in Syria. Here we see once more the ladder picture with the climbing and falling monks, as on our icon, and in addition an indication of the local setting: the monastery and the Virgin in the Burning Bush.

117

155, 156, 159, 160

115

The fourth among the richly illustrated books is the 11th century codex of the so-called "Christian Topography" of Cosmas Indicopleustes, i.e. the Indian navigator. In this treatise, attacking the Ptolemaic system, the author argues that the earth is flat and he tries to fortify his view with quotations from the Bible. The illustrations are of two different kinds. First there are illustrations from the Bible which he obviously copied from biblical manuscripts such as the marching of the twelve tribes with the ark of the covenant according to Chapter X of Numbers. The other type of

164–167

167

picture is schematic, showing the flat earth with a high mountain behind which the sun disappears and reappears and above the earth the firmament in the shape of the ark of Noah. These strange looking constructions were of course invented by the illustrator of the first manuscript in the 6th century, Cosmas who lived in Alexandria.

Compared with the wealth and variety of icons and illustrated manuscripts, the monastery has a rather meager collection of liturgical objects, far less than one would expect of a wealthy monastery. Apparently objects in precious materials, which surely once did exist, were plundered, melted down, sold, or presented as gifts to high dignitaries. Yet among the pieces which have survived a few are worth mentioning. A chance discovery from the period of the foundation of the monastery is a bronze cross of considerable size with an inscription incised in beautiful letters and an engraved design with Moses loosening the sandals and receiving the tablets. Placed on top of the late iconostasis in the chapel of the Forty Martyrs (Holy Fathers) the delicate engraving was only recognized after the cross had been studied from the top of a ladder. Because of the subject matter it is quite likely that this cross once decorated the main iconostasis of the sanctuary and that the Moses scenes related to those done in mosaic above the apse.

It is a pity that no objects of any importance are left from the middle Byzantine period (843–1204) of which we have such splendid icons and manuscripts. Yet there are a few pieces left of the Crusader period, a crystal cross from Murano (Venice) and a Limoges enamel with Christ enthroned nailed at the great entrance door. The continuity of Sinai's relation with the West is documented by a beautiful Gothic chalice in silver

and enamel, a gift of the French King Charles VI with a dedicatory inscription that he had it made as a gift for St. Catherine's monastery in 1411. This truly royal gift has the fleur-de-lis engraved on all its sides.

There are a few remarkable works of Islamic art preserved, reminding

158

us of the fact that Sinai is also a holy place for Moslems and that in front of the Church there is a mosque of the Fatimidic period still in use today. In it there is an elaborate mimbar or pulpit, and a Kursi, a stand for the Koran, both handsomely carved in wood. And in the gallery there is a beautiful aquamanile in bronze also from the Fatimidic period (10th–12th centuries). 141

If the treasure of the monastery, most of whose objects are now displayed in the gallery room of the new tract, still gives the impression of opulence it is almost entirely due to rich gifts of the Russians from the 17th–19th centuries which are often more ostentatious than artistic, though this judgment must be qualified. There are a few very excellent pieces of Russian jewelry like an encolpion with a beautifully carved cameo of St. Catherine — framed by enamel and pearls, of the kind 139 produced in the Kremlin workshops.

In spite of all the losses, what remains at Sinai of icons, manuscripts and objects, makes the monastery, a unique treasure house in which there exist some masterpieces of almost every century. They have contributed much to the enrichment of our picture of Byzantine art in general.

170 Ephgenios, the Economos of the monastery, leafs through a book. During our work a monk was always present acting as supervisor. They used the time to read.

172

171 Sacks filled with grain are hauled up into the monastery by the Bedouins.

172 The monks sorting the corn. A job that takes many days. Each sack is emptied onto a table to search for stones, since many a person has broken his teeth on monastery bread.

173

174

173 The ancient corn mill. It is still used to make flour.

174 The bread loaves are stacked on boards.

175 Monks and Bedouins make large rolls from the dough. These are then cut into sections and formed into small loaves.

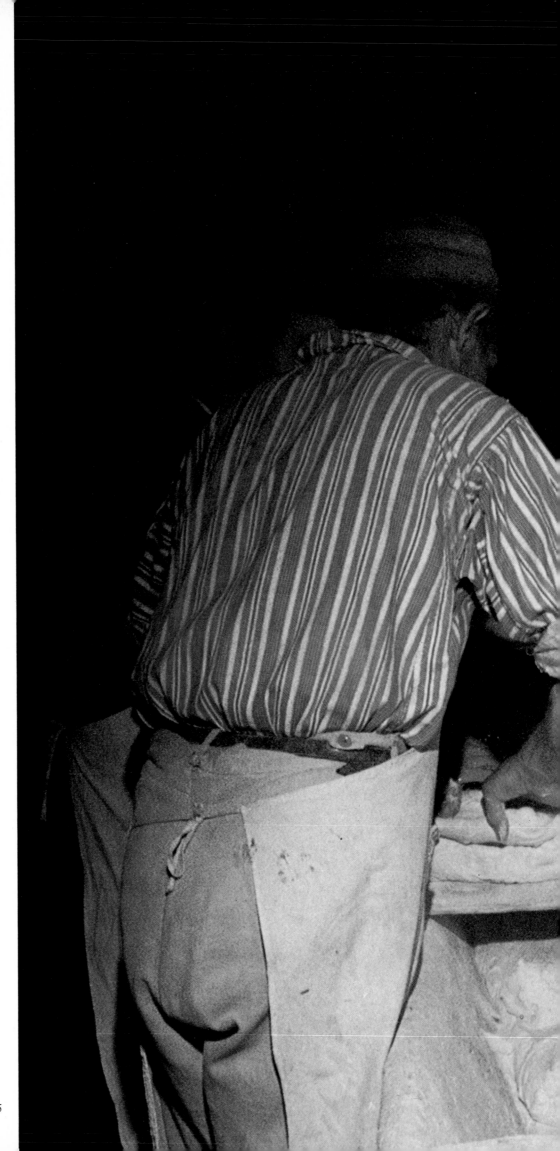

177

177

176 The bread is baked in the monastery's oven.

177 Some of the loaves are decorated using old wooden stamps. These loaves are used during church service.
(above) Bread with stamp of Mary, Mother of Christ.
(below left) Stamp with the burning bush.
(below center) Two stamps with the image of Saint Catherine.
(lower right) Stamp with monastery of St. Catherine.
(center right) Two stamps with initials.

178 The archbishop, His Beatitude Damianos, who normally resides in Cairo.

179 Father Jeremias at the church portal.

180 Father Nikandros, head of the Sinai monastery.

181 Father Ephgenios, the Economos, responsible for the household.

Father Dionysios,
guest monk, who
an active part in
work of the expe-
on.

183 Father Andreas,
always good-
humoured.

184 Father Spiros,
who rang the church
bells every day.

185 A younger monk,
a Greek from Alexan-
dria.

186

186 His Beatitude, Porphyrios III, Archbishop of Sinai from 1926 until his death in 1968.

187 Following service several monks talk at the top of the church's flight of steps. The name "James" is chiselled into the steps.

188 After their death only very few dignitaries can be kept in one of these alcoves in the ossuary.

189 The monastery cemetery holds only a few graves. This means that the oldest grave is dug up when one of the monks dies, the bones then being kept in the ossuary. The dry, warm climate prevents decay, the corpses dry out in the graves. Later, the "mummy" is carefully divided and the bones are put on specially prepared piles.

190 Stephanos, a monk from the sixth century, who used to guard the arched gateway, still keeps watch at the entrance to the ossuary.

188

189

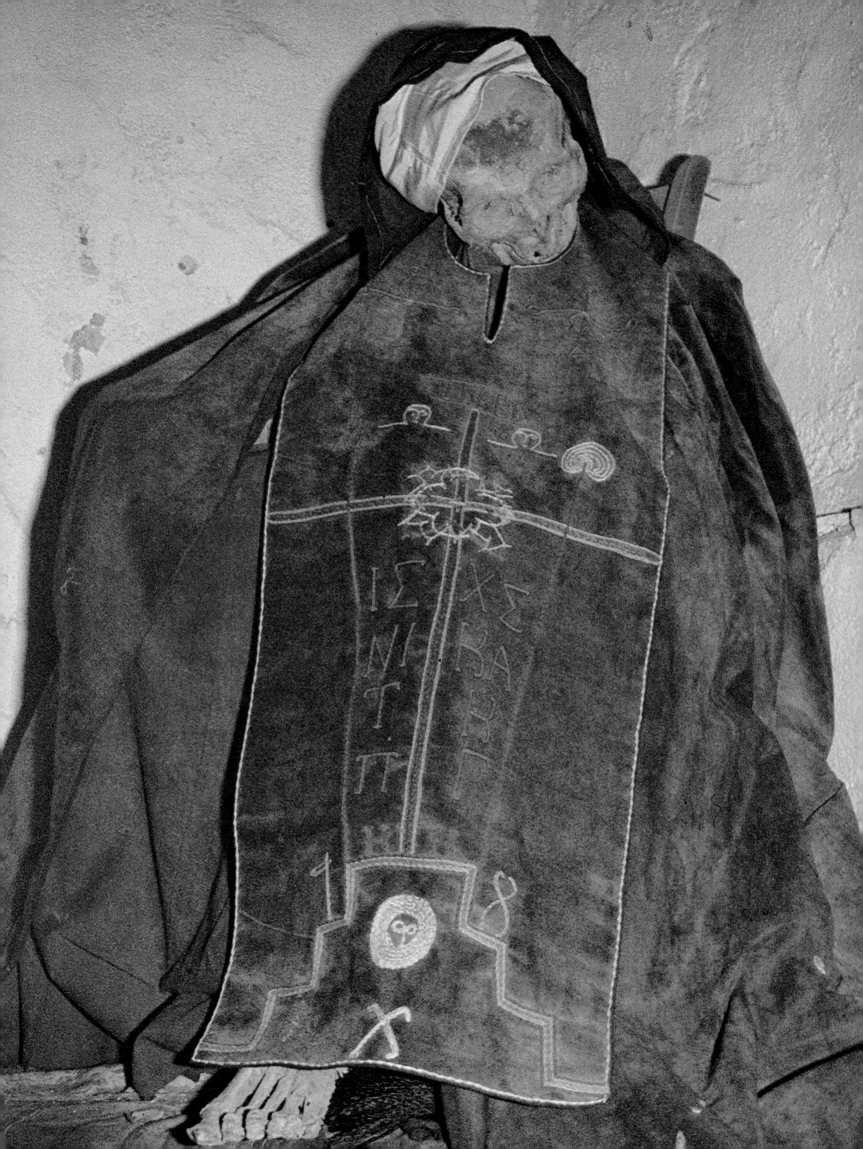

191 In front of the monastery Bedouins wait with their camels for our expedition. They are to lead us to Mount Sinai. A scene that has probably remained unchanged since 1,000 years.

192 This Bedouin girl, still a child, will soon grow up and hide her face behind a veil for the rest of her life.

192

193 The youngest daughter of our Bedouin, Saad, leads a thrifty but nevertheless unburdened life in the desert.

193

191

194

195

194 Three Bedouins chatting in the desert.

195 Saad, our dark-room specialist.

196 "Ful" – beans are the chief nourishment of the Sinai Bedouins. Flat cakes (left).

197 Baking bread – Bedouin fashion. A thin dough, rolled by hand, is placed onto a strip of metal. This is then placed over the fire. The tasty bread is ready 5 to 10 minutes later.

196

198 Saad's mother (left), his wife (right). The scarf is held by a plait, knotted in the front. The older the women get, and the more respect they command, the more facial jewellery they wear.

199

199 The author positioning an icon for an open-air picture in a chapel outside the monastery.

200 Photographing icons with electronic flash and large camera in a chapel of the monastery.

201 Saad developing colour films in our monastery darkroom.

202 Working in the library. Manuscripts are being photographed at right, icons at left. Electricity is supplied by the expedition's own generator (2,500 watts).

200

202

201

203

203 Professor Kurt Weitzmann (Princeton University) discussing an icon with Archbishop Porphyrios III (center).

204 Open-air picture of an early manuscript. From left to right: Moussa, my helper, Professor Weitzmann (Princeton University), and Fred Anderegg, chief photographer.

205 Professor George H. Forsyth, architect, director of the Kelsey Museum, University of Michigan, surveying the monastery.

206 A picture of the sky at night above the monastery. The camera is aimed at the Pole Star. Exposure time was six hours so that the stars formed circular patterns. The thin, bright line from below left to above right is the American balloon satellite "Echo 1." Below right is the silhouette of the Sinai range. A picture made possible by the dust-free, clear desert air.

207 The comet Ikeya-Seki, which was visible in the East over a long period of time at about 4 a.m. This celestial phenomenon looks like a biblical omen.

Appendix

NOTES

1 English translation by M. L. McClure and G. Herbert in M. L. McClure and C. L. Feltoe. *The Pilgrimage of Etheria* (London, 1920); concerning Mt. Sinai, pp. I–II.

2 *De Aedificiis* V. viii. I, 4–9 (English translation from H. B. Downey, *Procopius*, VII, Buildings Loeb Classical Library, 1954, pp. 355, 357).

3 *Est eciam in capitello eiusdem monasterii locus, ubi rubus stabat, ab omnibus tam Sarracenis quam Christianis veneratus .... Rubus quidem sublatus est et inter Christianos pro reliquiis distractus .... (Mag. Thietmari Peregrinatio. Ad fidem codicis Hamburgensis* Ed. by J.C.M. Laurent [Hamburg, 1857]). Laurent notes that the *capitello* is the *capitio s. presbyterio, ubi altare situm est (op. cit.* fn. 503). If it were possible to excavate in the area where the Bush originally stood, perhaps some traces might be found of the original architectural arrangements around it, such as retaining walls, balustrades, etc. Quite understandably, however, the monks would not authorize excavations anywhere within the walls of the monastery and certainly not under the floor of the Burning Bush Chapel!

4 *Buildings,* II. ix. 4–5 (Loeb, p. 157). Procopius is referring to the pre-Justinianic wall of Rusafa (Sergiopolis).

5 After the reading of the paper a commentator asked if the architect could not have found a solution which would place the church at least on the main axis, if not in the center, of the fortress. This is a point well taken. The answer, I believe, is that an architect working in the Roman tradition probably would have done so, somehow, but that the Mt. Sinai plan was made by a designer sensitive to the Greek tradition. In dealing with large complexes of important buildings the Greek tradition is more flexible and organic than the Roman, more concerned with the changing viewpoints and the vitality of diagonal planning (Delphi, Athenian Acropolis, etc.) than with the forensic confrontation of symmetrical balance which appealed to the military and legal mind of the Roman. In the situation at Mt. Sinai a Roman architect might have been inclined to impose a plan like that of a Roman camp by rotating the fortress rectangle counter-clockwise so as to align its main gate with the axis of the church. As noted above, any such solution would have projected the northeast corner of the rectangle far out on the valley floor, necessitating construction of a great protective bastion—a real levee—at that corner. The actual designer has taken a more typically Greek approach. Rather than contradict the natural configuration of the valley, he has accepted it and has thereby achieved a diagonal and descending approach from the main gate to the church. Such a leisurely, varied approach is not dramatic, but conduces to thoughtful appreciation of an architectural composition and of its meaning.

6 Viewed superficially, the masonry appears at first to be an ashlar of accurately faced and squared blocks having random lengths and an average height of 0.60 m. with flush joints carefully pointed, smoothed, and then struck with a sharp instrument so as to produce a rectangular grid outlining the blocks. Actually, the stones are dressed only on their faces and the real joints, behind the pointing, are large and rough hewn and are chinked with pebbles and chips. The interior of the wall, between its dressed outer and inner faces, consists of rubble stonework in abundant mortar, almost a flux of concrete. The wall structure answers, therefore, exactly to Vitruvius' description, five centuries earlier, of the Roman version of ἔμπλεκτον work (Book II, Chap. viii, 7).

7 *Visit to the Holy Places of Egypt, Sinai, Palestine and Syria in 1384 by Frescobaldi, Gucci and Sigoli,* translated by T. Bellorini and E. Hoade (Publications of the Studium Biblicum Franciscanum No. 6, Jerusalem, 1948), pp. 59, 112.

"There you see a fair large Church, covered with Lead..." This observation concerning the Mt. Sinai church was made in 1658 *(Theve'not's Travels into the Levant* in John Harris, *Navigantium atque Itinerantium Bibliotheca* [London, 1705], Lib. II Cap. IX, p. 433). In 1851 the nave of the church had a lead covering, as shown in a photograph made in that year by the grandfather of Mr. A. H. S. Megaw, to whom I am most grateful for a copy of this valuable record, almost certainly the oldest surviving photograph of the church. It may have been covered with lead from the beginning, like the Martyrium at Jerusalem which, according to Eusebius, was roofed with that material (H. Vincent and F.-M. Abel, *Jérusalem,* II [Paris, 1914], pp. 159, 208). As a possible alternative to lead sheathing, the Mt. Sinai church might originally have been roofed with tiles *(tegulae* and *imbrices),* which were in general use at that time on churches of Central Syria (H. C. Butler, *Early Churches in Syria,* ed. and compl. by E. B. Smith [Princeton, 1929], p. 199), but the large number of tiles required to cover the roofs of the Mt. Sinai church surely would not have disappeared utterly. In such a remote situation, where every piece of imported building material has always been precious, at least the *tegulae* would have been carefully saved for use as bricks in later constructions. I have found, however, no trace anywhere in the monastery of reused tiles. The massive balks of the trusses over the nave seem designed to carry such a leaden load as they ultimately were called upon to support. A modern roof of galvanized iron now covers the nave and aisles; the domes at the east end and the flat roofs of the side chapels are surfaced with cement; but the apse is still covered by sheets of lead on battens which rest directly on the half dome, constructed of granite blocks.

8 The texts of the three inscriptions appear in a preliminary publication by Prof. Ihor Ševčenko, which anticipates the full-scale study he will devote to them in the forthcoming volumes on the Monastery (I. Ševčenko, "The Early Period of the Sinai Monastery in the Light of its Inscriptions," *Dumbarton Oaks Papers,* 20 [1966], pp. 255–264). As to the Stephanos inscription, one of the problems in translating it is which of the English terms, "architect" or "builder," is more appropriate to express accurately his professional competence (in the inscription he is described as the τέκτνα). Pending the outcome of Prof. Ševčenko's future study, it may be safer to use the term "builder" as being less fraught with modern overtones than the term "architect" (cf. Downey, pp. xiv–xv in "Introduction" to Procopius' *Buildings,* as cited, *supra,* in fn. 2). As to the abilities and status, including possible ecclesiastical titles, of Syrian architects, see J. Lassus, *Sanctuaires chrétiens de Syrie* (Paris, 1947), pp. 262–264.

9 Ernst Kitzinger, "Mosaics at Nikopolis," *Dumbarton Oaks Papers,* 6 (1951), pp. 101f.

10 Elsewhere I have suggested that such may have been the case in St. Peter's at Rome as originally constructed ("The transept of Old St. Peter's at Rome," *Late Classical and Mediaeval Studies in Honor of Albert Mathias Friend, Jr.* [Princeton, 1955], p. 65). For a later example, probably to be dated in the fifth century, see fig. 48 herewith; the excavators found that the *schola cantorum* extended at least halfway down the nave from the apse. In general, see R. Krautheimer, *Early Christian and Byzantine Architecture* (Harmondsworth, 1965), pp. 76, 159.

11 A. H. M. Jones, *The Later Roman Empire, 284–602. A Social, Economic, and Administrative Survey* (Universty of Oklahoma Press, 1964), II, pp. 837–838, 1015.

12 A commentator on the paper said he felt it had drawn too sharp a distinction between the monastic and pilgrimage functions of our church, whereas there was an iconographic link between them since the Burning Bush has been considered an antetype of the Metamorphosis. Such a comment is very valuable in helping us to arrive at a just balance between the importance of each function and at the intended relation between them. At least the Bush and its pilgrimage were not accorded a monopoly of interest, as at Qal 'at Sim 'an where the adulation of the mere column on which St. Simeon had once stood came pretty close to fetishism and was far removed from the lofty Christian doctrines so subtly set forth in the Mt. Sinai mosaic. In this mosaic the Bush plays a role, but only a subordinate one, while Moses plays a major one, secondary only to that of Christ. Moses is the only person to appear three times in the mosaic. First, he is shown receiving his mission from God at the Bush; second, he receives on the summit of Mt. Sinai God's covenant with Israel, embodied in the Law; and finally he appears in the apse as a supporting witness to God's new covenant with mankind through Christ. The first two events had occurred nearby and seemed to be deserving of visible commemoration. Not only did Justinian build the monastery at the site of the Bush; he also erected on top of the mountain a chapel, now entirely rebuilt but incorporating reused architectural details which are recognizably Justinianic. These two memorials, like documents in stone, attested to two events in the unfolding of God's plan of salvation. But the plan itself, in all its vast sweep, was spread out above the high altar of the monks in the church which Justinian had built for them "so that they might be

enabled to pass their lives therein praying and holding services".

A question which deserves further discussion is the curious fact that Procopius asserts the church was dedicated by Justinian "to the Mother of God" and yet she is represented in a very subordinate position in the mosaic (in the medallion in the right spandrel of fig. 35).

Perhaps Procopius was wrong, which seems unlikely in the case of an important imperial foundation; perhaps there was a change of dedication while the church was under construction, but such a change would require an explanation. Any suggested solutions would be very welcome.

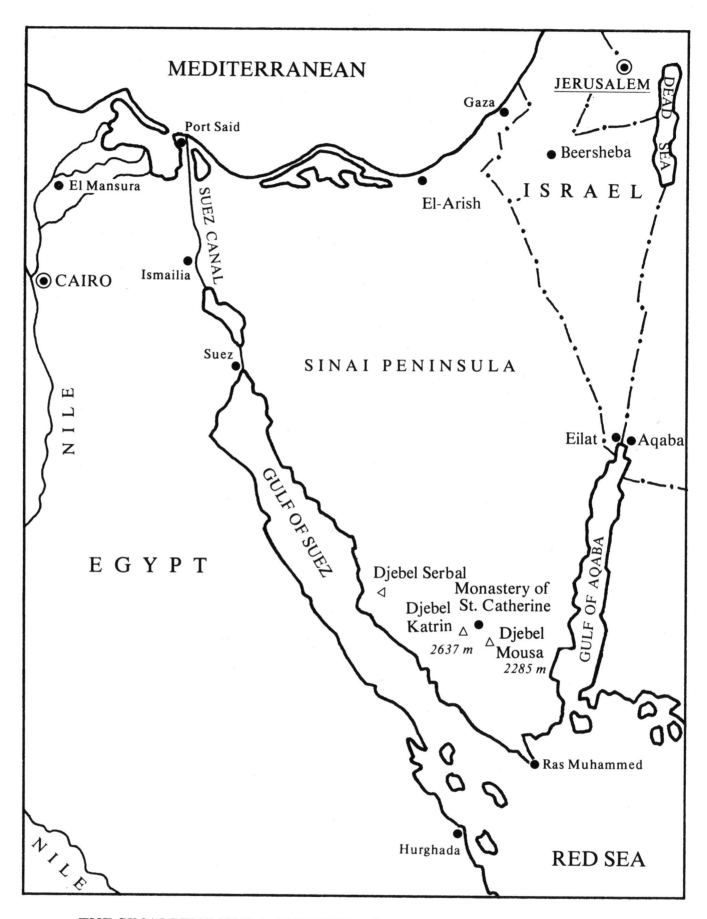

THE SINAI PENINSULA AND THE MONASTERY OF ST. CATHERINE

Index of Names and Places

Numbers in italics refer to illustrations